Dear Leslie "où sont les neiges d'antan" – enjoy the journey through the book – with love + appreciation of my story 1.3.12

The Magnificent McDowell

TRINITY IN THE GOLDEN ERA

Edited by

Anne Leonard

ECCLESTON PRESS

THE MAGNIFICENT McDOWELL

Dr RB McDOWELL LL.D

Professor, Emeritus Fellow and Junior Dean
of Trinity College, Dublin

© Anne Leonard, 2006
The Magnificent McDowell

ISBN 0-9553891-0-0
978-0-9553891-0-8

Published by Eccleston Press
4 Eccleston Square
London
SW1V 1NP

A CIP catalogue record of this book
can be obtained from the British Library.

Set in 11 on 13pt Sabon

Cover:
The Junior Dean in Library Square
Watercolour by
Rosalind Mulholland

Book designed & produced by:
The Better Book Company Ltd
Forum House
Stirling Road
Chichester
West Sussex
PO19 7DN
Printed in England

Contents

I ~ The Magnificent McDowell

II ~ Trinity in the Golden Era

III ~ Recent Encounters with RB McDowell

ACKNOWLEDGEMENTS

I am most grateful to the Board of Trinity College Dublin for permission to reproduce photographs from the film, *Building for Books*; and Charles Sweeting, Columnist of *The Union Jack – 'America's only National British Newspaper'* – for reminding me about this film, photographed in College, in the late 1950s.

I wish also to thank Rosalind Mulholland for her beautiful watercolour, *'The Junior Dean in Library Square;'* a companion to her previous work, *'RB McDowell in the Long Room'*; Eric Waugh for his phrase *'The Magnificent McDowell,'* the title of his review of *The Junior Dean – Encounters with a Legend* for the Belfast Telegraph; W.L. (Bill) Webb for his phrase *'A Revolving Happening'* and Joe Goy for his phrase *'Historical Giant'*, the Irish Times – with special thanks to Esther Murnane at the Irish Times Library – for photographs of RB McDowell and extracts from RB McDowell's correspondence with Joe Conneally, the Stanford family for permission to print an extract from 'Mahaffy' by W.B. Stanford and RB McDowell, the TCD Publications Committee for permission to print extracts and photographs from *Trinity News and TCD – A College Miscellany*; the AudioVisual and Media Service (Photography) TCD for its permission to print a sketch of The Long Room by Bryan de Grineau; Michael Gleeson for use of the College Seal, Richard Northridge for his photograph *'Returning to the Rubrics,'* and Charles Larkin for photographs taken during Dr McDowell's 90th birthday celebrations in 2003 and at the naming of the Boat Club's new boat, the *RB McDowell*, in 2005.

Others whom I would like to thank for their help and encouragement while I was preparing this volume are: Dr Robin Agnew, Pauline Brereton (Goodbody), Michael Brereton, Henry Clark, Beulah Garcin (Wells), Philip Garcin, Brian Lewis, Jennifer Lyons (Mrs F.S.L. Lyons), Lord Mereworth (The Hon. Dominick Browne), Jennifer Miller (Hart), Professor Martin Smith, Fran and Plotina Smith, Dr R. Andrew Somerville, Dr Richard Stack, Dr Brendan Tangney, Rob van Mesdag, Melissa Webb (Stanford) and Professor Trevor West.

I would also like to thank all those who bought or read *The Junior Dean* and everyone who sent material for *The Magnificent McDowell*. Their names, date of graduation and current whereabouts are recorded in both index and text and have been carefully checked – several times. 'Several times' because I am mindful of a warning by Dr McDowell, speaking at one of his multifarious birthday parties, when he said that he would not attempt to thank everybody who should be thanked. *'To do so'*, said he *'is to invite disaster – because you inevitably leave somebody out!'* Wise words!

As ever, all our thanks are due to RB McDowell himself, for providing, not only the inspiration for the books, but – from my point of view – for his act of faith in approving the contents, sight unseen. Any ordinary mortal, aware that people were writing about him or her, would ensure that they saw the results of such endeavours well before the book hit the bookshelves – but not RB! When I enquired whether he would like to take a look at the text, he declined. What would happen, he asked, if he spotted a mistake? There were, after all, bound to be plenty! Would he then have to start correcting them all? And if so, where would he stop?

Therefore, there has been no attempt to prove 'the truth' of any of the tales herein. The good faith of the contributors stands and the editor feels that she need take no further responsibility for the veracity or otherwise of the stories, given that, forty years on, even eye witnesses do not agree!

My final acknowledgement – forty years on –
must be to my parents who paid the fees
for my four amazing years at Trinity College, Dublin.

LIST OF ILLUSTRATIONS

Back Cover:

Leaving the Rubrics from a painting by Derek Hill
© The Executors of the Estate

Photograph of Anne Leonard
© Sheila Bailey (Kirwan)

COLOUR PLATES

From the film, 'Building for Books' 1958

TRINITY COLLEGE, DUBLIN (TCD) 1958

THE FAÇADE
>   View from Dame Street
>   View from Front Square

THE PORTERS
>   In Eighteenth Century uniform

FRONT SQUARE
>   The Dining Hall
>   The Chapel

THE (1937) READING ROOM
>   Exterior
>   Entrance
>   Filling out the slip in the Catalogue Room
>   Collecting books at the Desk
>   The Octagonal Interior

REGENT HOUSE
>   Junior Freshmen climbing the stairs to take the Oath

COBBLES
>   'The Well-Remembered Cobblestones'

CROSSING FRONT SQUARE
>   Processing from No. 6

CONVERSATIONS IN FRONT SQUARE
>   On the Reading Room Steps
>   On the Dining Hall Steps

Foreword

In 2003, when *The Junior Dean – Encounters with a Legend* was first published, it caused quite a stir: that morning, John Bowman had arrived with a camera crew to interview Dr McDowell for a television documentary; some weeks later, RTE produced a thirty minute radio programme on their 'Off the Shelf' series; 'Books Ireland' advised readers that everyone who knew RB *'must have a copy'*; Eric Waugh entitled his column in the Belfast Telegraph *'The Joyful Tome of the Magnificent McDowell*; Professor Trevor West wrote a half page spread for The Irish Times entitled *'Unholy Goings-on at Trinity'*; and Colonel John Blashford-Snell, writing in 'Sesame,' drew the attention of young adventurers to *'The Gun in Front Square.'*

One evening, a few months later, at a famous London club, a fly on the wall might have wondered why so many of the guests – during the address by a distinguished lady speaker – spent their time looking under the table, smiling. It transpired that, having just collected their copies of *The Junior Dean*, now hidden politely on their knees, they were totally unable to resist taking a peep at the contents. Yet, when I leaned across to see which of the episodes were causing such good humour, it was amazing to see that people were engrossed in the *'Index of Contributors!'*

JOSE XUEREB (1963) explains:

It was like being reunited with old friends whom one had not seen for forty years!

Soon after this, people started writing, or telephoning with further episodes that they felt should have been included in the book, prompting the question of what to do with all this new material. Turning to Dr McDowell I asked whether he thought that a second book might be called for, to which he replied:

'I'm not exactly bristling with feeling!'

Taking this for a 'yes,' I started work so that, now, just three years after *The Junior Dean* was published, *The Magnificent McDowell* makes its appearance, recounting even more episodes in the life of the most charismatic personality to have crossed Front Square during the greater part of the 20TH Century.

For most people reading this book – happily – our time there.

ANNE LEONARD
London, 10 October 2006
Anne@opnewworld.co.uk

The Rules of
Engagement

With the appearance of a second book of reminiscences about RB McDowell, it has been felt that it might be sensible to publish the 'Rules of Engagement.'

At the outset it was agreed that the editor and her subject should, while the work was in progress, keep at a distance from one another. This ensured that it would be impossible to suggest that the editor was being manipulated. This also meant that the subject, while very grateful and indeed flattered to be written about, would not be supposed to have authenticated anything suggested in the volume nor could he be held responsible for the veracity of any statement in the volume.

Anne Leonard   *RB McDowell*

Dr. McDowell's Path to the Reading Room

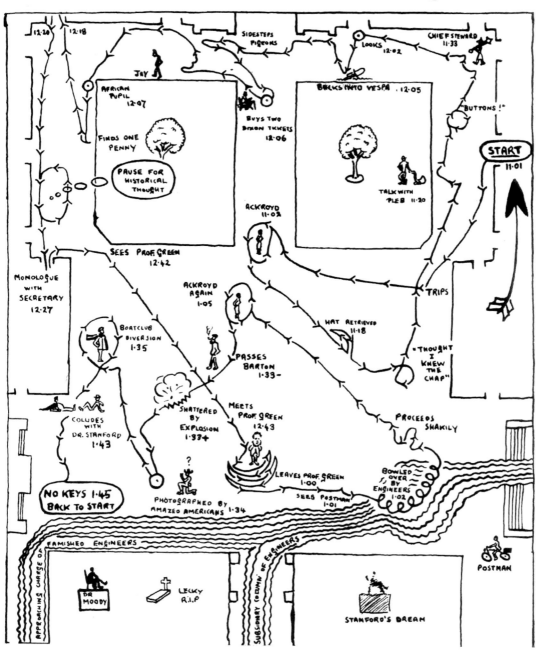

Reproduced by courtesy of the Publications Committee. This map appeared in *TCD – A College Miscellany* in November 1956.

I ~ The Magnificent McDowell

1

Tributes

They say that those who do impressions may be talented, but that the people they imitate are the true geniuses. Those who know Dr RB McDowell can be in no doubt as to his genius. Nor can any one of us who has not only known him, but also had the privilege to have been taught by him, be in the slightest doubt as to the enormous and everlasting impression he has made on us all. Dr McDowell – Thank you!

TERENCE BRADY (1961)

RB McDowell excels in his almost incredible ability to make and keep thousands of friends, not only among students and graduates of Trinity College Dublin, but all over Ireland and in England too. Being a Northerner himself, brought up in Belfast, RB McDowell personifies the unique position which TCD retains as an all-Ireland institution. It is a place where Catholics meet Protestants, Unionists meet Nationalists, and Northerners meet people from the Republic, become friends and, at least, to respect each others' views. For the future peace and prosperity of Ireland, North and South, few things could be more valuable. Professor RB McDowell, more than any other, has helped to perpetuate this unique Trinity College tradition.

HENRY CLARK (1950)

His exuberant flow of anecdote in private conversation shows the range of his reading and acquaintance, and the humanity of his spirit: it must have been splendid to be taught by him and he has always been exemplary in looking after the fortunes of his former pupils, so far as lies in his power. He is a great hearted man as well as a fine wordsmith.

PROFESSOR M.R.D. FOOT CBE,TD

I have known the incomparable Dr RB McDowell since he was a visiting fellow at St John's College, Cambridge when I was a student there in 1977. I was then about to embark on my writing career, during which he has been a constant and invaluable mentor and encourager, guide, philosopher and friend. I know I'm not the only writer to benefit from his wonderful interest and advice and for this reason alone, I feel he deserves recognition. But I know that he is also immensely distinguished in other ways, notably for his contribution over sixty years to academic life and historiography on both sides of St George's Channel.

MICHAEL BLOCH

RB McDowell has a deep love of Irish Georgian architecture. He has fortunately lived to see the Trinity College buildings transformed from blackened dirt-ridden grey stone to golden, pallid splendour. As a friend and fellow conservationist I commend and praise RB for all his lifelong efforts to preserve and restore the surroundings he loves so well.

THE HON. DESMOND GUINNESS (1980)

Many would say that RB McDowell was the most remarkable professor at Dublin University this past century. Former scholars and teachers will debate endlessly who the most influential don was, who had the most magnetic personality and so on, but no one would dispute that in terms of uniqueness, in terms of sheer unforgettability, there was none like him. As a scholar he is recognised as one of the great Irish historians of the late eighteenth and early nineteenth centuries.

ANDY O'MAHONY, RTE RADIO I 'OFF THE SHELF' 21/2/2004

Oscar Wilde said the Irish are the best talkers since the Greeks. RB McDowell is surely one of the best talkers since Oscar.

CHARLES SWEETING (1953)

It's amazing what affection McD has aroused among so many different people.

NIGEL PLATT (1950)

Simply put, he is one of the greatest characters that, in its span of four hundred years, Trinity has produced.

ERIC WAUGH (1952)

Trinity is fortunate to have such a distinguished figure, at the age of ninety-three, still living life to the full and presenting the human face of the university to the outside world.

PROFESSOR TREVOR WEST, FTCD (1960)

Most of what follows is true ......

Sketch of the Long Room of the Library by Bryan de Grineau

RB being interviewed by John Bowman
for RTE television documentary,
The Long Room, 13 September 2003
(l to r) Dr R B McDowell, Anne Leonard, John Bowman

2

90th Birthday

One morning in September 2003, tourists queuing in the Long Room to see The Book of Kells were riveted when they spotted a small dark figure darting through their midst, making his way, confidently, towards some television cameras. It was the eve of Dr RB McDowell's 90th Birthday and he was arriving to take part in a TV programme about himself. Waiting there to greet him were John Bowman, RTE's leading presenter, Dr Sean Barrett & Professor Brendan Kennelly – both ex Junior Deans – plus myself, clutching the first copy of The Junior Dean – Encounters with a Legend, to be presented to him, that evening, at a celebration in the Dining Hall.

The visitors immediately forgot all about 'The most beautiful book in the world,' mesmerised by the sight of the man in black who was by now being interviewed by John Bowman, filmed by the camera crew and photographed by the college photographer. They had no idea who he was, exactly, but everyone could see that he was very much at home – not surprising when you consider that RB McDowell has spent more time in that great room, climbing its ladders and reading its books, than any other man alive, while, with regard to television cameras, he had been a TV personality back in the 1950s when television was new and most of those watching were still at school.

Even from a distance, cordoned off behind the red ropes, the tourists could see who was in charge of the proceedings, while alert observers noted the deference, or was it reverence, or awe, on the faces of his listeners who only occasionally interpolated a bleat or two of their own. The visitors that day got a real bonus for they had been given a chance to see one of the most legendary figures in the entire history of Trinity. It was seventy-one years since he had first entered College.

The Belfast News-Letter, Wednesday September 17, 1913

BIRTHS, MARRIAGES, AND DEATHS.

Announcements under this heading are charged 2s 6d for 33 words and 6d for every seven words additional. Each announcement must be prepaid and authenticated.

BIRTHS.

MacDOWELL—September 14th, at Carrig, Bawnmore Road, Belfast, the wife of Robert MacDowell, of a son.

M'GOWN — On 13th September, at Dunsona, Derryvolgie Avenue, Belfast, to Mr. and Mrs. Melville M'Gown—a daughter.

90ᵗʰ Birthday
Senior Common Room, 13 September 2003
Patrick Guinness and RB McDowell

And almost ninety years since his début in Belfast where, on the morning of 17th September 1913, readers of the Belfast Newsletter learned of the arrival of their newest citizen. He was just three days old.

BIRTHDAY PARTY

Ninety years later, on the evening of 13 September 2003, a Birthday Dinner Party for RB, presided by the Provost, took place in Trinity.

Dr Sean Barratt, who organised the event, recalls:

At the dinner in the Dining Hall for McDowell's 90th Birthday, Andrew Furlong, former Rector of Trim and Dean of Clonmacnoise, presented RB with a signed copy of his book concerning his difficulties with the Church of Ireland. RB thanked him for

"A book by a heretic – I can smell the burning already!"

As we left the Dining Hall, after midnight, RB expressed his thanks for a splendid 90TH birthday dinner. I replied that he was the Junior Dean whom we all tried to emulate.

"Good of you to speak, Barratt, and quite brave. When I was eighty, Webb and Boydell spoke and they've both died."

DR SEAN BARRATT – JUNIOR DEAN (1986 – 2000)

The young RB McDowell

Courtesy of The Irish Times, 1957

3

Early Years

HOME

Robert Brendan McDowell was born in Belfast (where he still feels very much at home) and went to school at Inst. The McDowells had come from Ayrshire and were fairly rich business people who read the Belfast Newsletter which in Brendan's youth always carried the leading article from that day's issue of the Conservative British newspaper *The Morning Post.*

JOE CONNEALLY, THE IRISH TIMES 12.12.81

His family were Ulster Scots. They lived at 88, University Street. The house was straight out of Edward VII and the blinds were always drawn. I remember his mother drove around in a great big Austin 16. His father I never knew.

ALAN COOK (1955)

I was one of the ex-servicemen who came to Trinity after the War. The McDowells had been neighbours of ours in Belfast when we lived in Fitzroy Square and Brendan's younger brother, Patrick, was a great friend of mine at Inst. Pat joined the RAF and, sadly, was shot down in 1941. I remember their mother saying that he was totally unlike Brendan. But Brendan, of course, was an extraordinary person in his own right.

W.L. (BILL) TAYLOR (1941)

SCHOOL

When, as a young boy, he was taken by his respectable Malone Road, Belfast, parents to be interviewed for possible admission to RBAI, the then Headmaster asked young Brendan what he thought about coming to the school. After seven minutes of uninterrupted and anticipatory theorising, the Head said, 'McDowell, what would it be like if all the boys spoke as much as you do?' 'That would be a pretty kettle of fish, Sir.' He was admitted.

DR BRUMWELL HENDERSON CBE (1954)

His father was in business in Belfast and sent his sons to RBAI. At 'Inst.', RB McDowell was to become a member of a remarkable quartet of future Irish Historians. The others were T.W. Moody, D.B. Quin and N.C. Beckett. Between them they were to revolutionise the study of the subject.

ERIC WAUGH (1952).

Dr RB McDowell

I was fortunate that several of the masters with whom I was in contact at school were men with wide intellectual interests who were good, stimulating teachers, permitting lively conversation rather than practising more modern educational techniques. There was an excellent school library and, very close, was that great subscription library, The Linen Hall, where you could wander at will.

Trinity College, Dublin (TCD) 1958

In May 1957, a documentary 'Building for Books' was commissioned by the Library Extension Fund. Photographed in colour, the stills are reproduced here by permission of the Board of Trinity College, Dublin.

THE FAÇADE

View from Dame Street

View from Front Square

The Porters
In 18th century uniform

Once you had passed the porter's lodge and stepped into Front Square, you were in a different world. It was believed that the Gardaí's jurisdiction stopped at Front Gate and the porters, under the command of the Junior Dean, policed the precincts. Many were ex-servicemen, often great characters, who contributed between them many myths and legends to the annals of the Golden Era.

The Dining Hall

The Chapel

Exterior

Entrance

Filling out the slip in the Catalogue Room

Collecting books at the desk

The Octagonal interior

REGENT HOUSE

Junior Freshmen climbing the stairs to take the Oath for entry to the Library. As a deposit library, Trinity is legally entitled to a copy of every book published in Great Britain and Ireland. On entering College, every new reader takes the Seventeenth Century oath in which they declare that they *'Promise and vow faithfully'* to safeguard the books in the Library.

The 'Well-Remembered Cobblestones'

The feature which best typifies Trinity life is the cobbled expanse of Front Square. This is the hub of College life where one can stand and talk or just stand and wait.

TRINITY NEWS 5.6.1958

Processing from No. 6

Until 1957, ladies wore mortar boards and gowns in chapel. However, the Dress Code was changing and in 1958, Trinity News reported: *The recent removal of the regulations compelling ladies to wear mortar boards in Chapel means that no hat of any description is required to be worn now, although gowns are still obligatory.*

TRINITY NEWS, FEBRUARY 1958.

On The Reading Room steps

On The Dining Hall steps

Gowns were worn to all lectures

The Modern Languages Department, No. 35 New Square

On Commons: The Provost's Procession

For centuries, Grace has been said in Latin a memoriter *by a
Scholar of the House*

The Provost and Fellows arrive at the Examination Hall

Listening to the announcements

Tea at night

'Midnight oil'

ROOMS

A Party in Rooms

PLAYERS

The Revue
Players' Theatre, at No 3, Front Square

First sight of the questions

Opening Ceremony of The Manuscripts Room, 1957
Twenty years earlier, in 1937, De Valera had also opened the
Reading Room, seen in the background.

Scene in College Park, Trinity Week, 1958.

THE PRINTING HOUSE

*An unmistakable figure approaches
the Printing House, New Square*

UNIVERSITY

When RB sat the TCD Entrance Scholarship exams, the paper required candidates to attempt three questions. RB, however, got so carried away that he wrote only one long answer. The examiners, for their part, were so impressed that they ignored the letter of the rubric. They knew they were dealing with a young scholar of astonishing mental capacities.

DR RICHARD F.M. BYRN (1963)

This I was told by Geraldine Fitzgerald, then Librarian of the Representative Church Body of the Church of Ireland. She was an Historian and she had given grinds to RBD when he was an undergraduate. The grinds, she told me, consisted of him telling her, for fifty minutes, what he had read since his last grind, and ten minutes while she told him, 'Write so that the examiners can read it!'

JOHN TEMPLE-LANG (1958)

RB and I were Scholars on the same day, in 1936, and I sat beside him at the Scholars' Dinner. Later on, he always seemed pleased to see me on my occasional return visits. My only later memory – given me by an old school friend who also read History – was that Professor Constantia Maxwell said she would fail him in his degree examination unless he improved his hand-writing! He was a great character.

F.M. FOLEY (1937)

4

First Jobs

LIBRARIAN

One of RB McDowell's first jobs was as Librarian of the ancient Marsh's Library. He was Librarian there while preparing for his PhD. It was alleged at the time that, when engaged on his research, he would just put up a 'Closed' sign on the door of the Library so that he could work on, undisturbed.

PETER IRONS (1966)

RB McDowell was Deputy Keeper from 1939-44. I was told when I first came here – I don't remember by whom – that he was responsible for cleaning the vellum bindings in the Boutiereau Collection in the Reading Room. He made a good job of it – but to have let him loose with milk and water seems a bit risky. The Keeper himself has little to do and for the few years after 1957, when I was Deputy Keeper, I saw very little of him. My only memory can be of little use – he left his ragged scarf behind after one rare visit – to be carried back to Trinity – at arm's length!

DR MARY POLLARD (1965)

SCHOOLMASTER

When the war broke out, RB went to Radley College, Oxfordshire to replace staff who had joined the Forces. He made many life-long friends at the school, but it must be conceded that his somewhat unusual approach to teaching – later to enthral generations of undergraduates – more or less baffled the boys.

I remember him at Radley just before I got my School Certificate. He was always dressed in an extremely unusual way, with a scarf that was wrapped round his neck very tightly. He would come in and he would remove the first coat and then the second. He was completely from another world. In the class he taught, the boys were in total awe. Breathless, in surprise at him. I don't ever remember him giving us any work. He didn't engage the class and he didn't get any feedback from us.

RANDAL KINKEAD (1953)

The boys were horrid. We all mimicked him and threw bits of chalk. Looking back, I don't know how we were allowed to get away with it!

SIMON PORTAL, LONDON.

LECTURER

In 1945, RB McDowell returned to Trinity as a Lecturer. At that time, the English universities were struggling to find places for all the ex-servicemen who were coming back from the War, and, once the Oxbridge colleges were full-up, many people from the services and the English public schools, who might not otherwise have done so, found their way to Dublin. They took to the Trinity régime like ducks to water, providing an especially appreciative audience for Dr McDowell's amazing lectures.

RB's lectures were an absolute delight and were fully attended and were enormously racy. He would – in the same sentence – range over the centuries. For example, he would speculate 'I wonder what would have happened to Brian Boru's warriors at the Battle of Clontarf in 1014, had he had the rubber tyres invented by Dr Dunlop in Belfast many centuries later?' And it always seemed to be done off-the-cuff although occasionally a rather scruffy notebook like a child's essay book was to be seen. Such colour, light and speculation was expected from us, with similar responses in our examination papers, because he was interested in History in its major and wider senses rather than dates, names etc.

We wondered how he found time for the obvious reading and research that he performed. One explanation was when he confessed to us that he had been locked in the National Library all night and when we enquired solicitously if he had been alright, he replied 'Well, of course. I simply spent the night mugging up on a few subjects on which I was deficient. A most useful evening.' This from a man who had been incarcerated for a whole night with a solitary light bulb as companion and there he was at 10 am the next morning, fresh as paint, lecturing away, waving his arms, gesticulating, gown flapping and energy undiminished and all without breakfast.

DR BRUMWELL HENDERSON CBE (1954)

Unlike some others, McDowell's lectures were not often structured to give as many facts as possible. They intended rather to convey the flavour of the subject or age. I remember a particularly hilarious one on Laxists and Rigorists, Jesuits, Jansenists and Dominicans in the 17th Century, as exemplified in Pascal's Provincial Letters. And a comment, perhaps quoting Provost Mahaffy on c. 1900 Irish Society, 'An apothecary or an attorney was someone who might be invited to stay for tea, but would normally be expected to have left before luncheon.' Good story to amuse or baffle Americans or Scandinavians; and, of an 18th Century traveller in Italy who commented 'As it is Lent, the Court of Naples is closed, so the King hunts boars instead of receiving them.' A double test for any Continental's English.

CHRIS JOHNSTON (1966)

Though I was reading Mod. Lang., I had become friendly with a number of the Historians in my year, and when, in the course of one lecture, Dr McDowell announced that in (such-and-such a month and year) 'Brereton descended on Drogheda,' he was quite unprepared for the outburst of laughter that interrupted his flow and completely nonplussed him. Jubilant Historians told me the story as soon as they saw me after the lecture. I should point out, before anyone tries to apportion to me any sort of credit or blame for Cousin William's action, that one has to go back to the 14TH century to find the connection between us.

MICHAEL BRERETON (1961)

Dr McDowell held the post of Keeper of Marsh's Library from 1958 until 1979 and I recall a conducted tour that he gave to a small group of us from his Anglican History class in, I think, May 1965. I remember it was a gloriously sunny day, the place was flooded in shimmering light and we saw many ancient tomes, all emitting exquisite aromas wafted from past centuries.

PETER IRONS (1966)

TUTOR

I entered Trinity College in 1952 and RB, not yet Junior Dean, was my Tutor. One of my abiding recollections is of the untidiness of his rooms on the ground floor of No. 8, Front Square. Books and papers were dumped both on and under the table in the centre. Once I ventured to ask him how he ever managed to find anything. His reply was on the lines of: 'Well, at least I know what I'm looking for, is there!' A case of creative disorder, perhaps.

SIR RIVERS CAREW BT (1956)

A visit to his rooms for a tutorial was a nightmare. Books piled everywhere, the remnants of the odd meal yet to be tidied away, coffee cups all over the floor and nowhere to sit.

ROGER KYNASTON (1966)

A friend, Albert McMenemy, who graduated in History in 1971, had tutorials with the JD. A fellow tutee told him this one. He found it very irritating when Professor McDowell, during a one to one tutorial would keep throwing a pencil from hand to hand. This in itself was not so bad but every few minutes he would miss the catch and go shooting off into corners in search of the pencil. One day the said friend of a friend found himself facing Professor McDowell and noticed that the pencil he was throwing from hand to hand had a piece of string knotted around the blunt end. The other end of the piece of string was tied around Professor McDowell's waist. His curiosity got the better of him and he asked about this arrangement. The Prof. replied heartily 'Oh yes. Excellent idea. One of my pupils suggested it.'

DAVID QUINN (1973)

5

Junior Dean (1956 – 1969)

AN AMAZING APPOINTMENT

In 1956, when it was announced that RB McDowell had been appointed Junior Dean, most people thought that the Board had gone mad. However, it was soon clear that no Board could have taken a better decision for the new appointee rapidly became such a star, that, to people who were at Trinity at the time, and even people who were there beforehand, as well as the people who came afterwards, there could never again be any other, serious, contender for the title. Even today, they all still call him 'The JD!' And consider this: nearly fifty years on, a request to graduates for reminiscences about him has resulted in sufficient replies to fill two books – [so far!] A.L.

He was, at first sight, an unlikely man for the job.
PROFESSOR TREVOR WEST (1960)

I nearly fell off my perch when I heard he was JD!
ERIC WAUGH (1952)

I thought that he would be no good. Even useless.
How wrong I was!'
DR CHARLES HAYTHORNTHWAITE (1950)

'How wrong' indeed.
In less than a month the metamorphosis had begun.
Trinity News reported two arrests:

THE MAN WHO NEVER SLEEPS

On October 1ˢᵀ a new Junior Dean was appointed. Dr McDowell, a very familiar figure in Trinity, is a lecturer in History. He already has shown proof of his abilities as Junior Dean in several spectacular arrests. Notably, he apprehended several gentlemen the other night who had felt it right and proper to set fire to the cellar in No. 7. Known by the natives of Trinity as 'the man who never sleeps' it is likely that many of the night activities which so enlivened last term will be curtailed. Already one enterprising undergraduate has been caught entering the GMB at 3 am 'to have a game with the ghosts.' The prospect of finding that the helping hand which guides you to the last-foothold is that of the Junior Dean must daunt any Campanile climber.

TRINITY NEWS 1.11.1956.

He was probably the first Junior Dean to run after miscreants and try to catch them!

PAULINE BRERETON (GOODBODY) 1961

To my generation's thought, RB was an extremely unlikely choice for Junior Dean but, by all accounts, he seems to have been uncharacteristically efficient and judicial.   I suspect that he took himself off on one of his many trips elsewhere to refresh his ever flowing well of wit and wisdom to learn from contemporaries in the disciplinary field what would be involved for him as Junior Dean.

DR BRUMWELL HENDERSON CBE (1954)

AT PARTIES IN ROOMS

Soon after arriving at Trinity, I was told that the amazing figure seen chatting, dashing and jangling his way around Front Square, was the 'Junior Dean'; that he was a Fellow of the University, a 'Gold Medal' Orator, an academic of awesome intellect, an eminent historian, a famous television personality and so in demand, on account of his dazzling conversation and wit, that his presence was de rigueur *at every great house in the land; also, that his endless chattering was due to his voice attempting to catch up with his brain. Soon after hearing all this and while still a very new and nervous Junior Freshman, I was startled out of my wits to find him standing beside me at a party in rooms. There was no one else in sight. Having, at that time, little idea how to address so eminent a personality – especially this one – and to cover up my stage fright, I selected some peanuts from an array on a nearby table and timidly held out the plate. 'No thanks,' said the Great One, 'I'm not a monkey!'*
A. L.

The first undergraduate I met told me the Junior Dean had said that girls could do anything in college rooms so long as we did not let off fireworks. I promised that I would not let off fireworks. However, at the first party in rooms that I went to, I was worried when it passed the proscribed hour for going home, until someone said that it was all right to stay on, so long as the Junior Dean was still there – and sure enough – there he was, talking amusingly and at length to a circle of enthralled listeners. And therefore I thought that the Junior Dean must be in sole charge of life at Trinity.

JILL MCEVEDY (1961)

I used to have glimpses now and then of the JD rapidly disappearing round corners. But one day I did have a closer encounter when a male friend, whom I happened to meet in Front Square, brought me along to a party in rooms in honour of a sportsman who had won a race for Trinity. I was a bit taken aback to find that I was the only female present, but our well-mannered host seemed to take my presence for granted. Anyway, before long an emphatic voice was heard ascending the stairs, and in came the JD. He stood in front of the fireplace and speculated for about three minutes on the discomforts that runners must have to endure and then, suddenly departed, talking to his host all the way down the stairs. I was impressed, not just by his eccentric behaviour, but by the genuine and kind interest he showed in this sporting event. I have always remembered this scene and I know it was to my advantage.

MARJORIE CHAMBERS (DOUGLAS) (1962)

ON THE STEPS OF THE READING ROOM

BUGGERS v. BASTARDS

A small group of us had gathered on the platform between the two sets of steps up to the old Reading Room, the traditional spot for those taking a break from their books, the smokers to have a quick drag and the rest by contrast to get a breath of fresh air. The JD was suddenly of the group and the desultory conversation livened up. At some point, *à propos* of I don't remember what, the JD launched into a discourse on the sensitive issue of who you could safely call buggers and who bastards:

'You can call a state-school man a bugger as he won't see anything wrong in it whether he is one or not, because the lower classes etcetera etcetera. You should not, however, call him a bastard as you will be casting an aspersion on his parentage that, since he is lower class, may very well be true, and either way you are insulting his mother, so you could find yourself facing a very angry animal indeed. (In these days of Political Correctitude this view may need some modification). But a public school type should never be addressed as a bugger as it is all too probable that the monastic ethos of his educational establishment might have led him to dabble a little in that area or at least develop an interest, and he could very properly take offence at the reminder. But it's perfectly alright to call him a bastard, as being a public school type he will have no worries about his parentage and will recognise the term as an endearment or bit of upper-class cant.'

We must all have employed the word in such a way at some time or other: Pintlethrust, you old bastard, how have you been keeping?' 'Winkworth you old bastard' though not, absolutely never, 'McDowell, you old bastard...' Such familiarity would have been quite inappropriate from an undergraduate – the JD's expressed opinion notwithstanding. Sadly the old Reading Room is no longer in general use, having been annexed by the scientists or engineers or some other specialist lot.

MICHAEL BRERETON (1961)

The following encounters are believed to have taken place in the Fifties. We have three reports:

One story, current in my time, was of a female undergraduate who met him on the steps of the Library and stopped to ask him about something or other. After conversing for a few minutes they parted. Almost at once, the girl heard her name called. She turned back to hear Dr McDowell ask 'Could you tell me: when we met, was I coming out or going in?'

REV. H. BARKLEY WALLACE (1953)

My most vivid memory of RB took place on the steps of the Reading Room. With some others I was taking a breather from studying, and RB came up the steps and was accosted by a student with a request for some enlightenment on an historical problem. RB gave him a very thorough answer and then asked us 'When I started talking to that student, was I going in or coming out?' 'You were going in'. 'Oh good, then I have had lunch!'

REV. CHARLES COOKE (1954)

I remember passing him on my way to the Reading Room. He was just finishing a conversation, or perhaps a monologue, with a student and I heard his parting shot, whilst his keys whirled round his forefinger 'When I met you, was I coming in or going out?' At the time this seemed incredibly funny. As the years pass, both Roger and I can feel certain sympathy!'

VICTORIA HUDDLESTON (GOODBODY) (1960)

Solution: I can almost persuade myself I heard that particular McD story from the lips of one to whom it happened. *Probably it was a revolving happening.*

W. L. (BILL) WEBB (1953)

IN FRONT SQUARE

Front Square, once called Parliament Square, hides behind its austere grey walls a veritable hive of activity for anyone prepared to linger awhile. Enhanced by the presence of the Campanile, the Square is well known as the favourite hunting ground of Dr McDowell oscillating between No. 9 and New Square – that is, when he isn't oscillating between the Reading Room, the Catalogue Room and the Bursar's office – but that's another story.

TRINITY NEWS 7.2.57

I remember a delightful experience, which I enjoyed on several occasions, walking around Front Square while he speculated on how the builders of yesteryear might have constructed the lovely College buildings. Among the observations were 'The man who did the top of the campanile must have been fearfully brave'. Hours passed, seemingly in minutes, as he delighted with what was almost thinking aloud.

DR BRUMWELL HENDERSON CBE (1954)

NUMBER 9

The JD always did that strange waiting on the steps. One assumes that he needed to think where he had intended to go, sometime before.

BRIAN LEWIS (1964)

NUMBER 4

My only anecdote is in bad taste. It was said that someone leaned over the top of a cubical in the gents in No. 4 when he was inside and he rushed out, trousers around knees exclaiming 'The machine's broken down, the machine's broken down!'

DEREK FIELDING (1952)

IN THE READING ROOM

He labours for hours in the Reading Room 'Reading books' says Ron at the desk, 'faster than any man I know'.

TRINITY NEWS, 23.2.61

I quote my sister, DR MICHELINE SHEEHY SKEFFINGTON (TCD, Botany,1976), who compared Dr McDowell's progress around the Reading Room to that of a paramecium. This is a bit of a biologist's in-joke, I'm afraid, but no one who has ever observed a paramecium down a microscope and seen its constant, rapid and apparently random movement, will fail to appreciate it.

DR FRANCIS SHEEHY SKEFFINGTON (1967)

AN EPISODE OF NO IMPORTANCE

For years, people were able to tell and re-tell tales about RB and their own part in the scholarly skirmishes, unchallenged. However, once The Junior Dean – Encounters with a Legend *had been published, the various versions could be compared. Disconcertingly, the 'facts' varied quite wildly. Take the tale of the ladder from which Dr McDowell is reputed to have fallen – in the Fifties or was it in the Sixties – in the Reading Room, or in the Library – escaping injury or not, depending on the narrator. To complicate matters, RB now declares that he never fell off a ladder – it must have been Professor Moody.*

However, not everyone agrees! …

I can faithfully promise that I was actually present when RB stepped off the ladder in the Reading Room, date c.1953 or just before or just after.   The noise was deafening. Looking somewhat startled, he made a rapid exit, apparently unhurt. You may prefer to keep this to ourselves! Indeed, given his obsession for not dwelling on the past, he may have forgotten the incident for more interesting ideas!

DR CHRISTOPHER PETIT (1956)

I must admit I was a bit in awe of Dr McDowell and was often flummoxed when he sat down beside me in the Reading Room to make notes in the largest handwriting I have ever seen by anyone. I was even there the night he stepped backwards off a library ladder in the balcony of the Reading Room. Being young, we gave no thought to him being perhaps seriously injured – we silently smirked, confirmed in the fact that he was distrait and the perfect example of the absent-minded professor. Fond memories of the Golden Era!

SANDRA WEST WANG (1968)

Mortifying to discover that the episode of the library ladder is just legend (in the Reading Room, and he wasn't injured). But when I got to the bit where RBMcD explains that it actually happened to Moody, I'm sorry to say I grinned knowingly to myself.

DR RICHARD BRYN (1963)

RB McDowell
'The real trouble is people telling a story to improve it!'

AT PLAYERS' REVUE

Several of your contributors referred to McDowell as an ideal subject for impersonation and such was the case on stage at a student concert in the 1960s. The item was dramatically curtailed when (apparently) McDowell himself rushed from the audience to very sternly berate the actor for his impertinence. The animated harangue, however, was cut short, and then continued, by another 'McDowell' who appeared from the wings, soon to be followed by several others, all increasingly angry. I don't know whether any of them were authentic, or even whether the real McDowell was even present. Also, I am not sure whether or not this item predated the well-known sketch involving a multiplicity of Alan Wickers which appeared in a Monty Python show.

DR CLIVE WILLIAMS (1965)

Ned Darling, later Rev. Edward Darling, Bishop of Limerick, did an imitation of RB at a Trinity week Revue. He came on, pursuing a retreating student, in front of the curtain, between two items on the programme – it was an unannounced item. RB was in the audience at the first performance and was heard to remark that *'They could have allowed me to come on as an encore.'*

REV. CHARLES COOKE (1954)

We all tried to imitate the JD's voice and mannerisms, but of course none of us succeeded anything like as well as Terence Brady, whose take-offs were absolutely masterly.

PROFESSOR MARTIN SMITH (1962)

According to RB McDowell, the students' stories about him are mostly apocryphal but he does admit that the British television actor and writer, Terry Brady, portrayed him excellently in the annual college revues by the student drama group Players.

THE IRISH TIMES 12.12.81

RB McDowell

I really thought I was staring into a looking glass when I saw Terry Brady: he was rather like me physically and not only did he capture my voice perfectly but he caught my sentiments as well. I would point out that his monologue was extremely good. In my opinion, at least as good as my conversation – you know what I mean – it was intelligent.

THE BOAT CLUB

I recall his appearances at college balls, usually with a good-looking girl, and at the Boat Club.

DR JOHN CONNOR (1958)

On arriving at Trinity I was invited to a cocktail party at the Boat Club at Islandbridge and during the evening was introduced to the Junior Dean. I think I spoke to him for a few minutes before being distracted by another drink, or fresh talent. The following week I was parking my car outside the Old Stand only to notice the Junior Dean approaching, walking along the pavement. He looked quizzically at me, not sure if he could remember me; in the intervening moments he inadvertently walked into the lamp post! Polite and courteous to a fault he raised his hat and apologised to the lamp post before continuing on his way.

COURTENAY THOMPSON (1966)

I have a vivid memory of a Boat Club Dinner at Islandbridge when a completely naked figure, probably a cox, dashed in one door and out another, pursued by several oarsmen. The Junior Dean's comment 'Good gracious – it's just like a painting of Dante's Inferno – souls in torment, in Hell!

BILL MASSER

A SURPRISING DISCIPLINARIAN

In those days, what was striking when you stepped into Front Square, was the peace and quiet of the place. The Junior Dean saw to that. And yet! Beneath the surface, much was going on and, with more than two thousand young people, all bubbling with energy, high spirits and testosterone, it was not as easy to control as it looked. That the JD succeeded so well, with so little back- up, was amazing. How did he do it?

In the Mail Room – looking for the mail, 1959.
© *The Irish Times*

He kept us up to the mark!
CHARLIE WEBB (PORTER AT FRONT GATE 1956 – 1998)

Dr McDowell:
I took the duties of the office seriously. After all, I believe that discipline is the under-pinning of a university, but I did not allow those duties to absorb too much time. Most of the work consisted in giving permissions and advice as to how the concession should be used. A few times per year I had to deal with a minor crisis, usually the consequence of high spirits combined with an injudicious indulgence in wine. Undergraduates then accepted there had to be rules, allowed them to be imposed by their seniors, sometimes thought them to be silly and frequently broke them.

Dealing with the usual undergraduate *peccadillos* proved no problem for him. His judgements were fair and were readily accepted. With the arrival on the student scene of the Internationalists in the late 1960s demanding that the Junior Dean 'explain himself', and describing the College Board as 'lapdogs of imperialism,' things tilted somewhat against the JD.
PROFESSOR TREVOR WEST (1960)

Our formative years were touched by the JD's urbanity and one hopes that this has remained with one. I was, before my retirement at sixty, Dean of Higher Education at West Cheshire College, Chester, a validated college of Manchester University. It was a very daunting job and I came personally to understand McDowell's work in my more minor capacity. The problem is one of balance. I'm sure I did not get it right in the way he did. But I am not sure that he would have been able to suffer all the QAA rubbish that I had to fill in and account for, at every end and turn. So *The Junior Dean* book is very important because it gives a vivid picture of the civilised times in Higher Education before this plague we have to suffer called accountability. In fact the only accountability that has any validity is the one you have demonstrated by having received a plethora of testimonials to the JD's greatness.
BRIAN LEWIS (1964)

PRESCIENCE

All this was achieved with modest weaponry: he had the ability to admonish and the ability to fine, plus – the ace up his sleeve – his amazing ability to network. There was nothing and no one whom the JD did not know, or, more importantly, know about! He invited everybody he liked to his rooms for drinks and conversation, never forgot a name or a face and thus armed, could, uncannily, materialise at the scene of a crime even before the deed got under way.

Some time in my last year, the College had an experiment to replace the painted names of the occupants at the entrances of the staircases with a glass-fronted board which had slotted lines into which plastic letters could be stuck to spell out the names. The staircase chosen was the JD's own, No 9, a staircase that also housed Professor Stanford. This tatty substitute for the grand old traditional style of painted names had something of the effect on some of us that the infamous Bowl of Light (a cheap-looking, plastic, revolving illumination on O'Connell Bridge that was part of *An Tostal*, had had on Tony Wilson a few years earlier, when he had uprooted it and thrown it into the Liffey. We had no convenient river handy to throw the board into, but, once somebody had prised it open, it did lend itself to a happy re-ordering of the letters – not simply anagrams, but borrowing letters from anywhere on the board. We were busily engaged in this – Professor Stanford, I remember, had become Professor Pantsorf – when a porter arrived to inform us that we had been fined five pounds each. He pointed out the JD near the entrance to Number 2, who was gazing fixedly in our direction.

MICHAEL BRERETON (1961)

In the 1950s, three undergraduates – now very distinguished and too eminent to mention by name – discovered a trapdoor leading to a disused basement in New Square. The room was covered with cobwebs, dripping with damp and musty smells, but containing a capacious fireplace, large enough, opined one, for the making of Poteen, a popular if illegal beverage. The three agreed to instigate production, observing conditions of the tightest security, not a word to be breathed to a soul. And yet! The very next day, when they arrived to begin operations, there was RB McDowell waiting for them on the doorstep. 'I wouldn't do that, if I were you!' was his (unasked for) advice. To this day, nobody knows how he found out. A. L.

RB McDowell
I was brought up to regard Poteen as very dangerous!

FINES

The amounts, modest by today's standards, related, it seemed, not only to the gravity of the offence, but to the culprit's ability to pay up plus the alacrity with which he did so:

INSULTING PROFESSOR STANFORD   £5.00

There was a story recounted of one Commons, a proper term-time one, not one of the more casual vacation ones, when Professor Stanford, a striking figure with a head of steel-grey hair, was part of the progress to the high table. As he passed, one table or a fair number of the people at it started chanting 'Blue rinse, blue rinse!' The JD fined the whole table £5 a head.

MICHAEL BRERETON (1961)

GATE-CRASHING THE HIST.   £2.00

In 1962, when some girls gate-crashed a debate in the Hist., at that time a 'male only' preserve, the JD fined them £2 each for 'entering a place where they had no right to be'. A.L.

THROWING THINGS   (25p in new money)

'That will be 5 Shillings for throwing flour, Bermingham!'
TRINITY NEWS ......

THROWING THINGS AT THE JD   Negotiable

Jammy Clinch dropped a bag of water from No 18, Botany Bay, narrowly missing the JD. RB ran up the stairs and confronted Clinch who apologised, saying that he hadn't realized who he was bombing! The JD enquired whether Jammy had a car. He needed a lift to go down to the country and it was understood that the misdeed could therefore be forgiven.

DR CHRISTOPHER PETIT (1956)

ARGUING   Sliding scale

A man was fined £3. He protested. It was, he felt, too much. The Junior Dean re-considered, then announced: '£10!' 'What?' Pausing once more to reflect, the JD announced, '£15!' At last, the fined one 'caught on', scribbled a cheque for the initial amount and fled. It was as well to pay up.

ANON (1968)

RIOTOUS BEHAVIOUR   Unknown

I had to pay part of a fine levied by the Junior Dean on one who is now a very senior member of the College, following a riotous party in rooms. David McConnell was, at that stage, a student of mine and I hope he will not mind this occurrence being mentioned! The rooms were on the top floor of, I believe, No 34.

DR GILBERT HOWE (1964)

GENUINE MISTAKES   No Charge

I wonder who the understanding Senior Fellow was, who gave Dr McD the advice 'not to see things.' A sentence from one of Norman Lewis's books sprang to my mind as I read it: '*A successful officer gives the impression that he is forever overlooking causes for sternness.*'

The following incident occurred during one of my vacational sublets on the first floor in Number 2, probably in a summer or fair-weather spring vacation, as I had the window open. I had on a record, a rather jolly march that started with a choral section and then dropped the voices and carried on with band alone, when the fancy took me to go and buy something in the shop (on the ground floor of No. 10, beside the Chapel, in those days). As I crossed the Square, I was pleasantly aware of the faint sound of the singing following me. As I reached the shop, the voices finished their bit and the brass and drums came in with a bit more vim. But it was not till I was giving my order that the long *crescendo* began and memory popped sufficiently awake to remind me that the previous record in the stack had been rather a quiet one that had required the volume turning up and, additionally and more immediately, just how loud *this* record became towards the end. In an agony, I waited for my order to be filled, and by the time I came out of the shop, moving pretty smartly, the *fortissimo* was blaring round Front Square. Upturned faces were looking around and the Junior Dean, going like a startled rabbit, was shooting past No. 6 and into Front Gate. I broke into a run. Seconds later, a porter burst out of the archway like a hare with the greyhounds behind him, heading for No. 2. After that, only a cheetah simile would do justice to my sprint for home, and even then, the animal might have been hard put to it to match me over the last twenty-five yards. The porter and I reached No. 2 together, though without the head-on collision the ludicrous situation deserved. I gasped out some inadequate excuse-cum-apology: 'must have left it on … terribly sorry for *etcetera*.' The porter gave me a message to the effect that the Junior Dean required an immediate reduction in volume and I whizzed up to the room and lifted the needle from the disc, relieved that I'd got off that lightly.

MICHAEL BRERETON (1961)

There was the time he had to watch as David Dowse climbed up the front 'face' of Regent House, half plastered. RB was unable to say or do anything until he had made it to the top in case Dowse lost his foothold and fell …

DR JIM O'BRIEN (1961)

There was one incident when I observed the JD act with cool equanimity. It was high summer so the dusk was gathering, after we had all been thrown out of Jammet's or O'Neill's, or O'Donaghue's and David Dowse decided to go 'walkabout' on the parapet above the Front Gate. I heard the JD utter the instruction to the porters without fluster or stutter, 'Get him down' and they did.

DR JOHN CONNOR (1958)

Mere fines, however, paled into insignificance compared to the terrors of a reprimand. The JD's prowess in giving people a dressing-down was so legendary that, even today, the thought of being on the receiving end of one of his lambastings is enough to make a grown man quake. As Trinity News recalled, five years after he had retired:

For many years he was Junior Dean and a right ingenious one. Being an insomniac, n'er did he repose and when he suspected evildoings in the chambers of some luckless undergraduate, sharp would he knock on the door. When the wretched youth appeared, not once would the Doctor enquire what passed within or demand entry, but merely stand there for an hour conversing lively-like. When McDowell would finally leave, the boy would be too cold or wearied to return to his nefarious frolicking'

TRINITY NEWS 15.2.73

On one occasion I passed him in Front Square confronting a student, the latter almost squirming as his misdeeds were being laid out in front of him, and I heard just part of a sentence 'and at least *I assume – I assume –* that ...' Common politeness forbade me to pause to hear what was being assumed.

DR GILBERT HOWE (1964)

Former wrongdoers may be interested to learn of the existence of 'The Fines Book', carefully kept by the JD (and subsequently, by his successors) in which were recorded all misdeeds and that the tome remains, to this day, in the Manuscripts Room of the Library, where it may be inspected.

IN WHICH THE TABLES ARE TURNED

Only very occasionally was Dr McDowell out-flanked – but, alas, neither his famous fines nor his prescience could prevail against the daring, the originality and the sheer technical expertise of Andrew Bonar Law and his scholarly accomplices. In May 2004, Professor Trevor West – official biographer to the gang – wrote in The Irish Times:

THE BONAR LAW GANG

But it was the Law Gang under the inspired leadership of Andrew Bonar Law and his loyal number two, Brian (Shifty) Clarke (both scholars of the House) who caused the most disruption to the forces of law and order in Trinity during McDowell's tenure of office. '*Where will they strike tonight?*' was the Head Porter's pathetic cry. A famous occasion in the Examination Hall concerned an honorary degree conferring ceremony in which the Public Orator introduced the candidates with lengthy Latin orations which, it was generally felt, could have been drastically cut down. Some high-powered electrical engineering on the previous night had introduced a cable into the Examination Hall, hooked up to a switch in a nearby lecture room. The organ in the Exam. Hall had not played for more than a century but it struck up with a flick of a switch, playing Bach's *Passacaglia and Fugue* at full volume and completely drowning the Latin oration. This continued for a couple of minutes, then stopped – and everyone sat back.

The Public Orator resumed where he had been so rudely interrupted, but ninety seconds later, the organ struck up again, reducing the ceremony to a complete farce. Porters were sent up, by the JD, to the organ loft to arrest the organist and seize the record player which had been at the heart of the organ's revival. At last, the JD had a captive!

Professor Trevor West (1960)

EYE WITNESS REPORTS

Michael Brereton and Sam Maslin were in Front Square at the time:

The Music at Commencements incident that I recall did not have a player hidden in the organ! A speaker or speakers had been concealed in deliberately difficult-to-get-at place(s) in the Examination Hall, from which the wires ran out of the hall to where the player had been hidden in the basement of one of the staircases on that side of Front Square. It may have been a special conferral of an honorary doctorate on some Irish dignitary of the day. I was just coming out of Number 4, then the College 'Gents', to return to the Reading Room, when the music struck up; and even though I was out in the Square it fairly blasted me, so what it did to those in the Hall I dread to think. While I stood rooted to the spot by the din, porters appeared and went rushing in all directions trying to trace the leads from the speakers to their source. One went rushing by me into Number 2. But the music was not Bach's *Pasacalia & Fugue* of A B-L's report, not, that is, unless it features the theme of 'God Save the Queen' for that was what was issuing from the Exam Hall with all the gusto of what sounded like the massed bands of the Brigade of Guards could give it on a good day – and that at a time when the tune was liable to cause a riot on the streets of Dublin. The JD would, no doubt, have been directing the porters in their quest.

MICHAEL BRERETON (1961)

I happened to be crossing Front Square when the Exam Hall doors burst open and the JD appeared, looking hither and thither, for the culprit. I was informed at the time that it was Bonar Law. But then, Bonar Law was blamed for most things in those days!

SAM MASLIN (1959)

Professor West continues: Two days later the Junior Dean received a letter from the Gramophone Society informing him that its record player had been purloined and might have been used unofficially in the Examination Hall. The following day, he handed the record player back to the secretary of the Gramophone Society who, of course, was none other than Andrew Bonar Law. McDowell emerged from these and many other stirring contests bloody but unbowed.

PROFESSOR TREVOR WEST (1960)

AND, IN THE DISTRICT COURT

In the late 1950s, one of Basil Chubb's tutorial pupils was arrested for a minor offence and duly made his appearance in the list for the District Court. On the day, Chubb went along to provide moral support, in company with the Junior Dean, as guardian of the College's interest.

Chubb and McDowell settled down in the public gallery to watch the proceedings and waited for their man to appear. A succession of petty criminals made their way through the justice system, and to the growing irritation of the District Justice, the court was treated to a running commentary:

'Chubb, Chubb, cycling with no lights, five pounds? Five pounds – rather hard, don't you think?'

'Chubb, Chubb, our porters would have handled that faar *better than those guards!'*

'Chubb, Chubb, the judge doesn't like the look of that fellow!'

'I must say, Chubb, I wouldn't believe any of that!'

After several more of these contributions, the District Justice called for silence and addressed the gallery. History doesn't record the fate of Chubb's pupil, but the Justice made it clear that two Fellows of Trinity College were about to join him in the dock unless silence was observed.

Told by PROFESSOR BASIL CHUBB (1950) TO DR R. ANDREW SOMERVILLE (1972).

THE REGISTRAR OF CHAMBERS

The Junior Dean's duties were not, however, limited to discipline. He was also responsible for the accommodation – a daunting job, given that there were four hundred and fifty sets of rooms to be allocated and only four typewriters in the whole university. Amazingly, he succeeded in satisfying most people most of the time for he was always fair and could provide reasons for his decisions: for example, in the late 1950s, when Michael Leahy received a coveted set of rooms, all to himself, at the top of No 4, he inquired why he had been so fortunate when so many other people would have liked those rooms. 'You wrote and explained why you wanted them' *was the very reasonable reply*, 'No one else did so.' *A.L.*

BROTHEL IN RANELAGH

I lived in College during 1962 and 1963, so I was very much under his supervision. He had made me come into College to keep an eye on me since somebody had told him I was keeping a brothel in Ranelagh which, in fact, wasn't true. Three of us had a flat, without a landlord living downstairs, which was against the rules. It was simply that, Trinity Hall being in vicinity, but imposing, as did the College the regimen of a closed order on the women undergraduates, many were invited to tea. All we could deduce was that somebody under the influence of J.C.McQuaid* and his mates put the wrong two and two together and it got back. Hence the summons by the Registrar of Chambers.

BRIAN LEWIS (1964)

- *The Catholic Archbishop of Dublin who, in the Fifties, famously declared that it was a 'mortal sin' to attend Trinity. Fortunately, most people – especially those who had been at school in England – took no notice and enrolled anyway.*

SUB-RENTING

It was possible, in those days, to sub-rent a room from the regular tenant during vacations. Not much chance of doing that now, I gather, the times being very much a-changed. For these stays in College I could take advantage of the facilities and dine on Commons, for which I had to go and ask the JD's permission. It was, of course, always graciously granted.

MICHAEL BRERETON (1961)

Occasionally, there was a disagreement:

On one occasion I approached the JD at a student party about keeping my rooms for a further year. I'd already had three years in rooms, but had become a Chanter in College Chapel which had this advantage – as well as a small stipend. I got such a dressing down for daring to raise the matter with him there, that I left the party shaking. Dr McDowell wanted me out of rooms even more after he came to Chapel, on one of his very rare weekday visits there, and saw what I did for my stipend, which was £2.10.0 or £5.0.0 quarterly, I forget which. He said that I didn't need to have rooms in College just for this, but I pointed out that I didn't get them for free, and this perk went with the position. In a rather Irish situation, the Reader (the cleric taking the service) chanted, and the Chanter read the lessons.

COLIN P. SMYTHE (1963)

THE ROLE OF THE JUNIOR DEAN

The Junior Dean's office is one of the oldest in College and has been traditionally associated with the keeping of discipline. At times when spirits are high or political feeling intense, this can be a task requiring constant vigilance and abundant tact.

The office is traditionally held by a Junior Fellow and few incumbents have continued for more than one year but there have been a number of distinguished exceptions. Thomas Thompson Gray (a Cleric and a strong Tory) held the office with two short breaks from 1866 to 1892. His interest in military tactics may have served him well when coping with emergencies in Botany Bay. Sir Robert Tate ruled in the difficult epoch from 1919 to 1931. He displayed a firm hand and a sure touch and seemed positively to revel in presiding over disorder. His party pieces, which he would perform without undue pressure, included recitations of Kipling, and tap dancing (on a table). George

Wilkins on the other hand was a solitary man of caustic tongue who immediately upon his accession brought in the most stringent regulations, including lights out at an early hour. Immediate rebellion followed. Undergraduates paraded the College, pointing unloaded guns at the JD. The Fellows were required to patrol College at night in pairs until, having exercised relentless authority during November 1892, Wilkins was replaced by a more poplar man.

More recently, RB McDowell held office for thirteen years and may be regarded as the last of the long line of Junior Deans who were expected to enforce rules which would now be regarded as archaic. During his tenure, the custom of Night Roll was still observed. At a set time on each weekday evening, the Junior Dean, preceded by a porter with a lamp, would walk from his rooms to the vestibule of the Dining Hall, there to call the roll of College residents. The tradition has disappeared – for one thing, there are now three College gates open until midnight compared to only the wicket at Front Gate heretofore. The Junior Dean of today has different problems from McDowell's day, although of course the perennial ones remain.

PROFESSOR TREVOR WEST (1960) JUNIOR DEAN 1974 – 1978

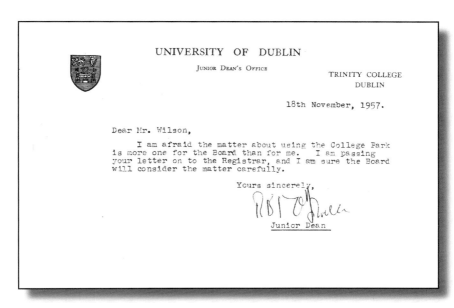

Request to fly model aeroplanes. Reply on page 49

'TCD – A College Miscellany' – 1971

6

Attire

A CERTAIN STYLE

Dr McDowell's apparel is worth a book in itself: on the premise that a gentleman should always wear a suit in a capital city, he embellished the basic outfit with a range of accessories – coats, scarves, cardigans, the hat, the glasses, the gown, and other items – sometimes all at once – in such a way that, winter or summer, whether in London, Athens or in Rome, you could spot him a mile off. What was the look?

My chief recollection is of his general sartorial ghastliness!
DR HENRY SMITH (1959)

I must have been a reasonably law-abiding undergraduate, because I do not recall exchanging words with Dr McDowell; but, even after some fifty years, I still have a vivid memory of him, overcoat, scarf, trousers at half mast, and above all, the hat which looked as if he regularly slept in it, and which rumour claimed he did.
THE REV H. BARKLEY WALLACE (1956)

Summer or winter, he was to be seen in his small flattened hat, waistcoat, and threadbare gown, always up for a bit of conversation. In fact, he could talk without pausing for breath for hours on end.
DR RICHARD STACK (1962)

A lifelong bachelor, he was not only a rumpled professor, he was chronically dishevelled, the same green hat and lengthy scarf, summer and winter. David Greene returned to Trinity, after many years, for a meeting at which Greene and McDowell sat on the same platform. Greene said that he was delighted to be back in Trinity and see so few changes. 'Why, even Dr McDowell was still wearing the same suit!'

CHARLES SWEETING (1950)

When I left TCD in 1949, I was more than aware of the developing legendary status of Brendan McDowell in his everlasting muffler and summer/winter overcoat. I drew the line, however, at his forty-nine blankets.

CHARLES BURROWES (1949)

This story was, I think, fairly well known in the Hist. at one time: Dr McDowell had agreed to propose the motion at one of the weekly Hist. debates. Came the hour: no Dr McDowell. A runner was despatched to the Rubrics to see what the problem might be, and found Dr McDowell deeply absorbed in reading, and oblivious of date or time. Reminded, he sprang into action, reached for the dinner jacket and black tie, and in five minutes bustled into the debating chamber, the haste with which he had changed being just visible to the discerning eye. The opening sentence of his address went something like this: 'Mr Chairman, Mr Auditor, Gentlemen of the College Historical Society, I may not be the best dressed man in Dublin, but I am the quickest dressed.'

DR FRANCIS SHEEHY SKEFFINGTON (1967)

Once, when he asked me back to his rooms after a debate at the Hist., I had a glimpse of his unusual personal habits. He had attended the Hist. in the required white tie and tails but I watched bemused as he peeled these off to reveal underneath the threadbare shirt, tie and waistcoat of his every day outfit. He had simply put one on over the other and thought this was perfectly normal.

DR BRUMWELL HENDERSON CBE (1954)

We had a debate one night in the Philosophical Society ("the Phil"). The JD was a principal speaker. When the debate was due to start, he had not appeared. There was general mumbling and we were beginning to wonder whether we should start without him when the door opened and he appeared. There was relief from the principal speakers involved in the debate, stifled laughter from the audience and the standard stuttered apology from himself. The JD was wearing his gown hanging off one shoulder, underneath was a formal dinner jacket and shirt with an untied bow tie and his ordinary daily trousers – and, of course he was wearing his trademark trilby – a man of fashion. The debate that night was a special black tie affair and we were all dressed up. Hence the JD's attempt.
CHARLES MULRAINE (1962)

Having moved into College rooms in Trinity Term, 1966, where I lived until the Summer of 1967, I used from time to time to attend College Chapel where it was the custom to wear a surplice – and hood, if appropriate – over one's normal clothes. One bitterly cold Sunday morning it was Dr McDowell's turn to read the lesson and he appeared, seemingly wearing a whole collection of pullovers, overcoats and scarves (but not, for once, a hat), the whole topped out with a surplice and doctoral hood and presenting the appearance of a sort of Michelin man. This, predictably, caused some mirth, but it turned into unrestrained laughter during the lesson itself which came from the book of Genesis. I can still hear that glorious voice declaiming the words 'Who told thee that thou wast naked?'
DR GILBERT HOWE (1968)

THE HAT

I had acquired a certain notoriety for impersonating him in numerous College revues and Dublin cabarets etc, imitations that he took with the greatest of grace and good humour. I even managed to obtain an original McDowell hat. Thrilled, I locked it away – only to be lectured by the JD the very next morning wearing – his hat. After the lecture I hurried to check my booty – afraid its rightful owner might have used my own tactics back on me – only to find the stolen hat still hidden safely away in my rooms. This led me to suppose the Professor had a never ending store of identical hats – or else – somewhere in Dublin Town existed a hat pusher – an illicit supplier of eccentric titfers to the gentry. And it was to him the good Doctor would hurry whenever one of his precious hats went AWOL. 'Ah, good day to you, Professor,' – the hat pusher would greet him. 'Dem wretched students been at it again, eh? The usual style, I imagine, – but what particular finish will you be wanting on it this time, Doctor? Slightly distressed? Bashed? Or altogether blathered? I tink we know the answer – altogether blathered certainly.'

TERENCE BRADY (1961)

Incidentally, John Pearson's reference in *The Junior Dean* to his dog pinching RB's hat does not tell the full story. It was a summer's day in the garden of John and Valerie. RB was in full attire as usual. Boris was at that time untrained and fairly wild. When RB bent down to stroke his head, Boris leapt and took the hat and ran around the garden frantically chased by John and Valerie with RB standing helpless in the middle of the lawn. Luckily, the hat was eventually rescued.

SIMON NEWMAN (1966)

One day, a friend, Carola Peck, who was coming to tea, rang to say 'I have a visitor who comes unexpectedly. May he come too?' Well, I got a great surprise when I opened the door. There, was this very unusual figure with a *rope* round his waist to hold his coat together. But he had charming manners and I remember that he never, never, stopped talking!

KATHLEEN WAY

TROUSERS

It's odd that in all the accounts of the JD's appearance [in *The Junior Dean*] none makes mention of the trousers at permanent half-mast, almost as defining a feature of his dress as the hat and scarf – though Chris Johnston's photo of him catches it exactly. It added to the impression one received of his being slightly airborne, as if he scuttled around an inch or two above the cobbles. None of us in those days would have had the presumption, certainly none of us would have dared, to ask him what he was in mourning for. But it's a nice fancy that he wore them so for the passing of the 18th Century view of the world.

MICHAEL BRERETON (1961)

TWO OF EVERYTHING

It would be a mistake, however, to think that the Junior Dean had only one set of clothes. He had many different outfits. It was just that, when he wore them, they all looked the same. Take the famous coat: there were in fact three; one for each of the capital cities in which he lived. This meant that people in Dublin saw the Dublin coat whereas in London or Belfast, people would see the coat designated for that particular city. London got the best one. What was confusing was that, sometimes, you saw two at once:

In the 1990s, RB came to Belfast to speak at the AGM of the TCD Association of Northern Ireland in Belfast and stayed two nights with my husband and me. He arrived wearing *two* black overcoats. He explained that he always did this when he was unsure of the weather, one coat being a winter one and the other more suitable for warmer weather. Wearing them both at once saved on the packing and left him flexible as to what to wear, day by day, during his stay. The rest of his apparel, including his dress suit, was in a holdall strapped to a little trolley, which he pulled behind him.

JANE WRIGHT (COOKE) (1966)

I have heard him talk for one hour and a half upon the importance of always carrying a spare pair of socks in case one's feet should get wet. He explored, he exhausted the subject. He described puddles he had fallen into in Ireland, in France, in Italy; in anecdote after anecdote he pursued his feet through all the mud of the civilised globe; wandering far but never losing sight of the point of his discourse, returning always to his ground-base with the grand chord-like words: 'But luckily, I had a spare pair of socks in my pocket at the time!' It was magnificent, like listening to Bach's 'Art of Fugue.'

TRINITY NEWS 22.05.58

THE GOWN

'But there was only, ever, one gown'

1940S

I well remember his *gown* – which looked like a collection of green, rather sludgy, pools and with which he occasionally cleaned the blackboard.'

DEREK FIELDING (1952)

1970S

Sometime in 1977-1980, I was crossing Front Square on my way to Commons. An agitated figure emerged from under the Campanile and thus from the direction of the Rubrics, also bustling to Commons. He trailed well down his shoulders a very greened and bleached worn lecturer's gown that eventually fell off onto the cobblestones. The figure continued in its haste, so I picked it up and caught him up, proffering the lost garment. I was greeted with an absent-minded but broad smile and the words 'Oh – thank you! They are so expensive nowadays!'

DR MICHELINE SHEEHY SKEFFINGTON (1976)

2005

In late 2005 I was invited to Commons by Andrew Somerville and to a pre-prandial sip of wine in the Senior Common Room. To my great joy, the JD was still there – almost forty years later – sitting by the fire, deep in The Spectator, clutching his gown. I engaged him in a little light conversation about Georgian Dublin, and then the call to Commons came.

'Here, Jordan, help me with this!' I suddenly heard – and there he was, standing, with one arm through one of the Gown's armholes, the other searching vainly behind in mid air for the other. Where was it, this hole? I looked, in vain, for lo, the Gown, equally advanced in years trailed behind us on the floor, with knots in it, for a full fathom and a half. I picked it up in the middle, searched feverishly, and failed! A crowd of jostling helpers started to gather, and much advice flowed. An agonising minute and a half later we were finally rescued by a senior member of staff who had seen it all before. A hilarious, but deeply moving moment, in the life of the Gown of three score years and ten.

CHARLES JORDAN (1963)

UNIVERSITY OF DUBLIN
REGISTRY OF CHAMBERS
WEST THEATRE BUILDING

TRINITY COLLEGE
DUBLIN

28th November, 1957.

Dear Mr. Wilson,

    The Board has decided that you *Club* may fly ~~your~~ model aeroplane in the Parade Ground.   Perhaps you could have a conversation with me about making arrangements to do this.

        Yours sincerely,

        Junior Dean

[From page 41] Reply to Colin Wilson's request –
permission granted.

Trinity Monday, 2002
© Charles Larkin

7

Academe

Dr R. B McDowell LL.D,
Professor, Emeritus Fellow and Junior Dean of Trinity College, Dublin

APPOINTMENTS

FELLOW 1951-1981

JUNIOR DEAN 1956-1969

READER IN HISTORY 1962-1967

ASSOCIATE PROFESSOR OF MODERN HISTORY 1967-80

ERASMUS SMITH PROFESSOR OF ORATORY 1980-1984

HONORARY LL.D, 2003

PUBLICATIONS

Irish Public Opinion 1750-1800 (1944),

British Conservatism 1832 – 1914 (1959),

The Irish Convention 1917 – 1918 (1970),

The Church of Ireland 1869 – 1969 (1975),

Ireland in the Age of Imperialism and Revolution 1790 – 1801 (1979),

(with D.A. Webb) Trinity College, Dublin 1592-1952: *An Academic History (1982),*

The Fate of the Ulster Unionists (1997),

Crisis and Decline: The Fate of the Southern Unionists (1997)

Grattan: A Life (2001),

Also essays in biography:

Alice Stopford-Green (1967), A Passionate Historian (1967)

(With W. B. Stanford) *J.P. Mahaffy, A Biography of an Anglo-Irishman (1971),*

'*Land & Learning – Two Irish Clubs*' (1993),

Editions of the letters of Edmund Burke and the journals of Theobald Wolfe Tone.

His most recent work, '*Historical Essays (1938-2001)* was published in 2004

A Tribute, by graduates and friends, entitled
'The Junior Dean, RB McDowell – Encounters with a Legend,'
was published in September, 2003
to celebrate Dr McDowell's 90th Birthday

The Magnificent McDowell – Trinity in the Golden Era
followed in October 2006,
marking the 50th anniversary of his appointment as
Junior Dean.

'HISTORICAL GIANT'

It is safe to say that McDowell is now the leading authority on 18th Century Ireland. But to say that is to leave out so much: the love of conversation, the stream of anecdote, the memory so magnetic of detail, the talent to call up word pictures of historical figures two centuries old as if he had just shared their lunch table.

ERIC WAUGH (1952)

He is the author of about a dozen books which put him in the front in rank of Irish Historians. We attended his lectures on Irish and British History, and he saw History as a Grand Sweep, as Tolstoy did.'

CHARLES SWEETING (1950)

He was not only well-versed in the voluminous (now there's a McDowellism!) detail of 18th Century political life – he could produce much of it from his encyclopaedic memory, referring effortlessly to names, places and dates with such a fluency that it sometimes seemed that he personally existed in that society more intimately than in ours – time-travelling – which some found absurd. Yet to some of us he conveyed, by the vividness of his enthusiasm

Dr RB McDowell 1981
© *The Irish Times*

and using scarcely any philosophical or moral comparisons, a sense of the reality of the past and its timeless relevance.

JOE GOY (1953)

For people interested in the study of late 18th Century history in these islands his most authoritative and most consulted works are those entitled *Ireland in the Age of Imperialism and Revolution* 1790-1801 (1979) and *Irish Public Opinion* 1750 – 1800 (1944). They are 'classics' and appear as authorities in John Ehrman's magisterial life of William Pitt the Younger Vol III *The Consuming Struggle* particularly with reference to Chapter IV.

The most striking appeal of McDowell's work is the depth and breadth of his scholarship. This is corroborated by the ease of his style and the sense of his profound interest in the variety of human experience conveyed through his prose.

One would expect, and receives in abundance, the wisdom and balanced judgement in his published work inherent in a scholar who has detailed knowledge of primary sources gleaned from his editions of the *Letters of Edmund Burke* and of *Irish Historical Documents*.

When he turns his pen to portray individuals, we are given deep insights into Wolfe Tone, Grattan and Sir William Rowan Hamilton.

Trinity College Dublin owes him a profound debt for recording and illuminating the past of the College not only in his captivating biography (with the late Professor W.B. Stanford) of Provost Mahaffy, but also, in his academic history (with the late Professor Webb) *Trinity College Dublin* 1592 – 1952 – *An academic history*.

In connection with Professor McDowell's prolific and influential publications, it is characteristic of the wide range of his historical interests to find a piece by him published in *Theology* concerning the social, educational and spiritual qualifications required over the centuries to be appointed an Anglican bishop.

BRIAN LEWIS (1964)

RB McDowell is the best sort of Historian: he writes about what he understands thoroughly, and illuminates every page from his own experience. His book on the Southern Irish Unionists, and their fate after they were abandoned at the establishment of the Irish republic, shows all the virtues of a well-constructed book on a highly controversial subject: there is nothing in it at which either a devoted Unionist or a devoted Republican can take offence, and yet it covers the ground so thoroughly that nobody has thought of re-attempting the task.

PROFESSOR MICHAEL FOOT CBE, TD

Re: Trinity College Dublin (1592 – 1952) by RB McDowell & DA Webb *Extract from a letter to Joe Conneally at the Irish Times, 2.12.81*

The new book is a history of Trinity College, Dublin from the foundation to 1952. My co-author is Professor D. A. Webb, the botanist. We have one definite advantage – our history of the college is the first to be written since the large collection of college muniments and other manuscript collections relating to its history have been reorganized and thoroughly catalogued. We have, too, what I hope are two other advantages. Each of us has been for fifty years connected with TCD and while Webb is a scientist, I have always worked in what I call the West End of College. The hard core of the book is a study of the academic aspects (presumably the most important) of the college – the courses, teaching and scholarship; but we have not neglected Trinity personalities or 'characters' (many, sad to say, now forgotten) and we have paid a fair amount of attention to academic politics and to Trinity's relation to the world outside its walls.

Having telephoned RB in London for further details, Joe Conneally wrote:

When Robert Brendan McDowell, historian, wit and television pundit of the Sixties, answered questions by telephone about the book which critics regard as his *magnum opus*, for a minute or two he could not remember the precise title of this seven hundred page work on eighteenth Century Irish History, which took many years of his life to research. Checking through the available files at his flat in North London, he quickly made amends, briefly explaining this temporary aberration with a typical McDowell remark which perhaps is reminiscent of a Trinity forerunner, Oscar Wilde, in its careless abandon: 'Once a book is finished, one loses interest in it immediately.' Yet behind the apocryphal stories and the revues, there was a distinguished academic career. This began with works on politics and public opinion in Ireland from the mid-eighteenth Century to the mid-nineteenth, then proceeded by way of the British conservative tradition to the Irish administration of the nineteenth century and to a History of the Church of Ireland from Disestablishment in 1869. He also edited Burke's letters and wrote an amusing biography of the Provost, John Pentland Mahaffy in collaboration with W.B. Stanford.

JOE CONNEALLY, THE IRISH TIMES 12.12.81

8

In His Own Words

RB McDowell
on
Politics, Writing,
Conversation,
Work
And
Himself

EXTRACTS FROM LETTERS TO
JOE CONNEALLY AT THE IRISH TIMES, 1981

ON POLITICS

I find it rather awkward to write about my politics. To begin with, I now realize that, although I have opinions and express them readily in conversation, I have never even written 'a letter to a paper,' let alone appeared on a political platform (The nearest I have got to action is a subscription to the Conservative Party). So, if I may say so, the best approach would be to put it indirectly: that is to say that it would probably be noticed by anyone talking to me at any length that my feelings are those of an Ulster Unionist, that my general political attitude is that of a moderate English Conservative, and that, although I am very happy in Dublin, and clearly have a great liking for many Dubliners, I am not (to put it mildly) very sympathetically responsive to manifestations of Irish nationalism.

ON WRITING

I find writing a distasteful chore. Crystallising my ideas and finding the right words is very tiresome. And only very occasionally is there the gratification of being able to say to oneself, 'THAT is a good sentence.' I suppose a sense of duty and an urge for self-expression keeps one going.

While by no means silent in conversation, I am a great believer in short, concise work in print. I am a great believer in slim books.

ON CONVERSATION

I realise that I have spent a remarkable amount of time in reading, writing and talking – conversation and lecturing – (some may say the distinction is not always apparent) and I would usually be described as talkative. Indeed, I enjoy conversation and when engaged, talk with application and energy. But when I consider my other occupations, by nature solitary, I don't think I devote an undue amount of time to talk. I would even be prepared to boldly argue that my 'talking-time' is under average.'

ON WORK

As regards my work, you can get a less biased picture from the members of the Modern History Department – several of the members, including the present Vice Provost, [Dr David McConnell] besides having been colleagues, were pupils.

ON BEING ASKED TO WRITE ABOUT HIMSELF:

It is one thing to write about myself on the assumption that no one will read what I have written for fifty years. It is another thing when I am aware it will enter into an article which may be read in the near future by friends, acquaintances and critics. It is hard not to pose so that the light falls right.

Thinking about yourself in a sustained way is a sobering exercise. In one mood, so much time and so little done. In another, swept away by waves of mild complacency.

9

Personality

FRIENDSHIP

I cannot remember how I met RB, though the year was probably 1948. On the face of it, we had little in common. RB was his famous self, erudite, a masterly raconteur and wit, and unmistakable, in the hat and the grey woollen rope-scarf, this, perhaps knitted by some inept female admirer. I came from the horsy squirearchy of County Waterford, but via Stowe, where perhaps I had gained a modicum of culture. Against my own wishes, I was now grappling with the aridities of Roman Law. In any event, we did meet, and I remember with gratitude many an evening in RB's rooms in Front Square. A bottle of claret would be warming near the fire, and gradually the evening light would fade, till the rooms became dark. Never was the electric light turned on – perhaps RB was in fear of an extortionate meter charge. Talk would be mainly of 19th Century Irish politics and of the few grandees who still survived, on their Munster estates. It was a great privilege of have become one of RB's circle. We still are in touch.

DR PETER DEMPSTER (1952)

The last time I saw him, I had been away from Dublin for at least ten years. But, for the JD, such absences simply don't count. I swear he picked up in the middle of a sentence! 'Oh, Richard, I was just wondering ...' as if we had seen each other the previous evening.

DR RICHARD STACK (1962)

VALOUR

I was appointed (or about to be appointed – I forget which) – as one of the first 'Assistants' to the JD in the last months of his office. It must have been at the end of his last Trinity Term as JD. I was reading in my rooms at the top of House 24 in the Rubrics, dimly and reluctantly aware of party noise that was becoming excessive from somewhere within No. 38. My sitting room overlooked New Square. I could see McDowell heading for the trouble. The matter was in safer hands than mine. He disappeared from view. A brief pause ensued, then a prolonged crashing, breaking roar of noise; then silence. I ran down the many steps and across to No. 38. At the foot of the stone stairwell – still emitting pings, twangs and groans, like a newly commissioned concerto for percussion and random silences – lay the crushed and disintegrating remains of a full size piano. In such circumstances one immediately looks for the edge of a grey scarf, a scattered trilby hat, a fragment of elderly gown, crumpled lecture notes, or an old shoe protruding from the circumference of the calamity. Then I looked up, in time to see McDowell slowly, bravely, but with awesome determination climbing the stairs to interview someone at the top. And the rest of the story of the piano that did not fly of its own volition is for someone else to tell.

PROFESSOR JOHN GASKIN (JUNIOR DEAN 1978 – 1983)

CHARISMA

He was already a living legend when I was at TCD, and that was over forty years ago.

PETER K STEEL (1964)

He was always a gentle soul albeit at times unconscionably frank to the point of disturbing the unduly sensitive. His many imitators, while occasionally recapturing part of the man, were never able to penetrate the mystery of how this apparently frail and not large person could radiate such hypnotic energy and never, ever, be boring.

DR BRUMWELL HENDERSON CBE (1954)

Some people of his kind, who have this personal dynamism, can spread their aura to people who have never known them closely, giving the impression and even conviction of having had a relationship with them. Psychology cannot account for it with any certainty.

BRIAN LEWIS (1964)

CANDOUR

To an annoying mother, vaunting the attractiveness of her son:
'Simply put, I believe that your son is being pursued
by women of both sexes'.

BRIAN LEWIS (1964)

George Sevastopulo from Geology told me the following story recently which he said had been recounted to him by Dr David Thomas, Director of the Student Health Centre. In the summer of 2004 RB called to see Dr Thomas who asked him directly to his office, bypassing a queue of students waiting outside.

RB: 'Thank you, David, for seeing me ahead of all these sick students'.

DT: 'Oh, they are not sick. They are medical students here for their hepatitis injections.

RB: 'Hepatitis! Is that to do with alcohol?'

DT: No – sex!

RB: 'Ah. I knew it was something pleasurable'.

BRENDAN TANGNEY, JUNIOR DEAN (2000 – 2005)

PHOTOGRAPHIC MIND

Before starting work on The Junior Dean, *I wrote to Dr McDowell to ask if he approved of the idea and he replied that, while he liked the concept of the book, he absolutely did not wish to see the text prior to publication nor become entangled in any details relating to facts. Long before there was any text however, I went to see him, (at the Institute of Historical Research), taking with me the first batch of correspondence, hoping – just hoping – that he might indicate which, if any, of the tales were 'off the wall.' But no. Politely flicking through the pages, but at unbelievable speed, like a card player in* The Sting *or* Butch Cassidy, *he put all the papers down, unread. I was disappointed, but then, I had clearly forgotten who I was dealing with, for he leaned back and was off, reminiscing about the contributors, even though I can assure you that he had not paused long enough to see the pages – let alone read any. It was a feat that had to be seen to be believed, proving that the JD can scan a page as fast as his hand can turn it.*
A.L

PRODIGIOUS MEMORY

One evening, in May 2004, some fifty years after he had graduated, Dr J.A.D. CLINCH, (1954) was crossing Front Square, when he met the erstwhile Junior Dean. 'Good evening, Sir,' said Jammy, 'I'm Clinch' 'I know that!' replied RB, 'You read Medicine.'

DR CHRISTOPHER PETIT (1954)

I saw RB at dinner early this month, that is, January 2005. A quite amazing example of his memory was his telling me exactly where and when, in Front Square, he and I had first met, in the very icy February of 1947. I had forgotten but it came back to me and he was 'dead on'.

HENRY CLARK (1950)

A niece of my wife, Ann, studying history at University, was staying with us last summer. Over the course of dinner one evening, she innocently asked if he knew anything about Cecil Rhodes. During the course of the next thirty-five minutes, RB gave her a detailed rundown of the history of Southern and Northern Rhodesia and the development of the mining industry in South Africa. The next day, passing Hampton Court, the same niece innocently asked if he knew the wives of Henry VIII whereupon he not only reeled them off in the right order but included a detailed account of what happened to each of them.

SIMON NEWMAN (1966)

PERFECT TACT

There has been a recent problem concerning the Boat Club rooms in Trinity which were at No. 23 for almost half a century. This arrangement was suddenly discontinued and I became involved in correspondence with the College authorities about the matter. Last Christmas whilst RB was staying with us, I showed him the file of correspondence and his comment after reading through it, was I believe, classic: '*I have read the file in detail and I believe I would have handled the matter in a different manner.*'

SIMON NEWMAN (1966)

My husband, John Kurkjian, and I, together with George and Diana Kurkjian and Dudley Staunton were staying at the Kildare Street & University Club on the sad occasion of the funeral of John Boland. It was probably on the Friday that the chaps wanted to watch the rugby downstairs and I decided to read somewhere quietly. The Club was deserted and I wandered through an open door into an elegant, comfortable room overlooking St. Stephen's Green and sank gratefully into an ample armchair in the corner.

About fifteen minutes later I was aware of someone entering, who proved to be Dr McDowell. Like a pointer, he made a beeline for me (I am sure he did not know me as it is my husband John who was at TCD) and after a kindly greeting he gave me to understand that I would be far more comfortable in the Drawing Room, where there were such attractions as MAGAZINES. He had clearly never seen a magazine, but he knew that ladies liked to read them and this would be an added incentive. I obediently followed and was duly delivered to the Drawing Room. It was only later that I realised that the Library door had been left open, which was why I had failed to see the *Members Only* sign.

CHRISTINA KURKJIAN

YOUTHFULNESS

'He never seems to get old, like the rest of us'
CHARLIE WEBB, PORTER AT FRONT GATE (1956 – 1998).

When I entered Trinity in the Fifties, I had the impression that Dr McDowell was very old! How stupid I was. I learned in Book One that Dr McDowell was born in 1913, so in 1951 would only have been thirty eight years old!!! That is YOUNG these days. So why did we think that Dr McDowell was OLD? Were we so brainwashed that we considered anyone over the age of thirty to be 'past it'? I am ashamed of that now, and, given the chance again, I would have a more adult approach to life.

SHEILA KANE (1955)

Of course in 1969 we all thought the Prof. was about eighty. The scarf worn in summer seemed to confirm advanced years. I was astonished when I saw Prof. McDowell in Holborn Tube Station about eight years ago apparently no older than he had been nearly thirty years before. I suspect a Mephistophelean contract.

DAVID QUINN (1974)

ECCENTRICITY

Reckoned to be the only genuine survivor of the 18th Century, one must search the pages of Lewis Carroll to encounter an equal. His eccentricity is mellowed with antiquity – contemporaries of the Junior Dean vouch for his unique behaviour'

TRINITY NEWS, 23. 02.61

No doubt RB McDowell, only recently retired from the aptly named Erasmus Smith Chair of Oratory at Trinity (conversation is his only hobby), knows that he has become one of the characters of Dublin through his eccentric, using the word in the strict classical sense of 'away from the centre' mannerisms and behaviour – his absentmindedness and dress (the woollen scarf is well remembered by RTE viewers and producers).

JOE CONNEALLY (THE IRISH TIMES 1981)

McDowell was on a bus talking to a fellow undergraduate. The latter commented, '*You don't seem to have shaved today, McDowell!*' to which came the reply, '*No – I shave only every few days. My wife, however, shaves every day!*' Caused a sensation amongst the passengers.

REV'D PROFESSOR E M NICHOLSON (1960)

One can never forget that roll-call thing at 9 pm when the porter, looking like a depressed jockey with his 'lanthorne', was followed by this phenomenon in a gown, mortar-board, overcoat and scarf, chattering away to itself, came to sign us in; worthy of Aeneid Book 6 in my view. After TCD, I went on, as it were, to King's College, Cambridge which had its crop of 'funnies', but nothing to touch him, so far as I could see. He turned up at King's as examiner for the PhD

and this entertained the librarian, Dr Munby, for some time.
BRIAN LEWIS (1964)

My memories of the JD are very vivid to this day. The photograph of him in *The Junior Dean* striding across Front Square in 1966 is just as I recall him. I remember him as an extraordinarily intelligent man with more thoughts going through his head than his mouth could cope with at one time!
SAM MASLIN (1959)

The Doctor (for such is his universal sobriquet) is a famous talker, most especially to himself, for he never walks but he talks, and the common people of the city watch in wonder as he promenades Grafton Street, absorbed in his own chatter, beating his way from his Rubricks Chambers to the University Club where he breakfasts daily on coffee and biscuits.
TRINITY NEWS 15.02.73

RB does not think of himself as eccentric. He does however quite like to be thought unconventional. Once when we met by chance in Dublin in the 1960s, he kindly invited me to dine on Commons at High Table. The main course was a leg of lamb and as soon as he was served, RB asked me to pass the mustard, remarking 'No one else will want it' and of course, he was right. We laughed over the old dictum that mustard with mutton is the sign of a glutton – a dictum which, after trials in private, I've concluded has more to do with the rhyme than with the flavour of the meat.
HENRY CLARK (1950)

Brian Inglis summed it up when he recalled RB as a lecturer in the late forties and stated 'No university could be regarded as 'conventional' which employed McDowell on its staff'.
TRINITY NEWS, 23 02.61

CAMBRIDGE RIVALS

There may have been eccentrics like the JD at Cambridge, but they covered it up by behaving like country gents. None lived in a 'cave' like his in No 9. At Cambridge there was a don called John Saltmarsh who used to make his own ink from glue and soot. If he invited you to a party, all your other mail stuck to his invitation card. The closest they had to our JD.

Then at Trinity College, Cambridge – where I was supervised for part of my time – there was an odd old don called Canon Simpson. A man asked him what he actually DID for all his perks and he replied 'I make myself available for conversation'. He had his own aeroplane and went about Cambridge with a pair of garden shears cutting off the branches that touched his hat.

BRIAN LEWIS (1964)

RB McDowell
'Mind you, I'm no expert on Lunacy.'

10

Multiple Roles

CELEBRATED CONVERSATIONALIST

He is a Belfast man with an eccentric dress code who speaks, reads and writes often at breakneck speed. A bachelor and the most sociable of men, he lives collegiate life to the full, and can speak knowledgeably and swiftly on an extraordinary range of subjects to the amazement of visitors to the college.

PROFESSOR TREVOR WEST (1960)

At Oxford, Sir Maurice Bowra was famed as a legendary conversationalist. Warden at Wadham College, scholar in Greek Literature, Professor of Poetry, Vice-Chancellor of the University and President of the British Academy, he had long been regarded as without equal for his fluency and wit.

In May 2006, at the Scholars. Dinner at TCD, the Provost told one of my favourite stories about RB (who was of course present). The Oxford side of the story can be found in Hugh Lloyd-Jones's (editor) volume of essays by friends of Maurice Bowra published by OUP in 1972, *Sir Maurice Bowra 1898-1971*. The essay records an evening when Bowra – Warden of Wadham – was dining at All Souls and McDowell was also there as someone's guest. You will read in the essay how McDowell out-talked Bowra who was celebrated at that time as Oxford's greatest talker and one whose extraordinary range of knowledge could normally dominate any High Table.

I was present at TCD (then a lecturer there, I left in 1967 and I think this occasion can only have been a year of two earlier) when McDowell returned from this Oxford sojourn. We all knew that he had been at a dinner when Bowra was also present and we were all intrigued to know what clash there may have been between the greatest talker in all Ireland and Bowra. At lunch in TCD a day or two after McDowell returned, Stanford at the table began the conversation, asking RB how the Oxford trip had gone, had he seen old so-and-so, etc. Then he asked McDowell about hospitality there and McDowell let us know where he had lunched and dined, what debate he had attended etc. Stanford probed him about his dinner at All Souls when Bowra was present and then asked the question which brought silence upon the entire lunch table: *'How did you get on with Bowra?'* The reply was: *'Oh, he's a perfectly nice chap, but he hasn't much to say for himself.'*

THE REVEREND PROFESSOR E.W. NICHOLSON (1960)
FORMER PROVOST, ORIEL COLLEGE, OXFORD

ELOQUENT ORATOR

I dropped into the GMB to hear the Hist. Debate on the motion 'That Ireland should rejoin the Commonwealth.' The highlight of the evening was the spluttering oratory of Dr McDowell. What a brilliant effort this was! Speaking without notes, he regaled the audience with a feast of scintillating effervescent wit and cynicism, shattering the rickety structure of his opponent's arguments and providing an illuminating insight into the development of Irish social history.

TRINITY NEWS, May, 1967

GUEST SPEAKER

When he graced our company as Guest of Honour at a TCD Association dinner in Bristol back in the 1970s, he was in deep conversation (monologue?) with his immediate neighbour when called on to speak and he simply stood up – for twenty – thirty minutes – and seemingly continued with his train of thought, eventually saying that he had gone on for long enough and sitting down to unbounded applause.

DR GILBERT HOWE (1964)

What a colleague described in the TCD *Gazette* as 'A rich flow of observations punctuated with anecdotes that might have graced the more accomplished members of The 18ᵗʰ Century Parliament on College Green to whose interpretations his early studies were directed.'

TCD – A COLLEGE MISCELLANY, 1981

THE TRINITY MONDAY DISCOURSE: It was in the GMB, the Trinity Monday Discourse of 1980. Professor Woodhouse leant over to me and said 'Did I ever tell you I once heard David Greene and McDowell in Front Square lamenting that there were no characters left in Trinity?' But Provost Lyons was on his feet to introduce the speaker: 'My function this morning is more than usually superfluous. But choosing speakers for the Trinity Monday Discourse is a rather delicate operation – a little like touching the shelves of a good library. The shiny, new, unopened volumes tempt one to take them down; but occasionally you have a strong urge to select a comfortable, well-thumbed volume.' (Prolonged laughter). The Provost, a man of teasing humour but impeccable good manners, continues somewhat hastily, 'And I mean it in the highest sense as a compliment. This is the fourth Trinity Monday Discourse Dr McDowell has given and that is an index of the unending attraction he has for us all.'

Dr McDowell then spoke for forty minutes without hesitation, repetition, or apparent pause for breath, on Henry Grattan. In his words of appreciation at the end, the Provost observed that Dr McDowell belonged to that tiny minority who appeared to achieve perfect eloquence without effort: 'Eloquence seems to flow out of him like some natural force, but always disciplined and channelled by historical scholarship of a very high order'.

PROFESSOR JOHN GASKIN (JUNIOR DEAN 1978 – 1983)

THE MIRACLE OF THE ARTICULATE SLEEPER: In April 2005, at the instigation of the then Junior Dean, Brendan Tangney, a unique dinner took place in Trinity Hall. The company included all but one of the Junior Deans since 1956, and almost all of the Wardens of Trinity Hall since 1945. As the evening lengthened out, each one of us contributed some reminiscence of times past. McDowell appeared to have been asleep for some time when Trevor West, sitting next to him, asked loudly (and presumably, rhetorically) 'Anything to contribute, McDowell?' Within seconds, the sleeper was launched, seemingly unbriefed and certainly unwarned, upon a coherent sequence of well-structured paragraphs (with footnotes and references where necessary) picking up points raised by others and entertaining with new items of his own. He ended with an anecdote concerning an earlier JD, c.1944, memorable for idiosyncrasy not to be found again in later and more ordinary holders of the Office.

Putting together several fragmentary accounts the story appears to be – but I cannot produce any reliable documentary evidence – that a certain undergraduate returned to College one night exceptionally elevated by drink. He was followed across Library Square by the porters who observed him smashing several ground floor windows in the Rubrics. The porters called the Junior Dean. But by the time he arrived, the unfortunate young man had entered a staircase and was seen sitting on a second floor windowsill at the back, with his legs dangling out. The Junior Dean, perceiving the precariousness of the situation, remonstrated with him from the safety of the ground, urging him to get back inside while the porters made their way quietly to the room. But to no avail. The man lurched forward and fell; but in a very loose way on account of the amount of drink taken. He landed among bushes in the soft earth of a flower-bed, picked himself up, presumably in a somewhat shaken and sobered condition, and wandered off. Asked what retribution the Junior Dean proposed, he replied 'Since Providence has forgiven him it would be exceeding even my authority to do otherwise'.

The Junior Dean then sat down to prolonged applause for the same eloquence disciplined by scholarship that Provost Lyons had commended a quarter of a century earlier in the young man of sixty-six.

PROFESSOR JOHN GASKIN (Junior Dean 1978 – 1983)

MEDIA STAR

It is now sometimes forgotten that McDowell was one of the stars, if not the star, of early Irish television, appearing on a *Postbag* programme, where his self-assurance in front of the camera belied the pre-programme panic of the make-up team.

PROFESSOR TREVOR WEST (1960)

When I invited him to do some History programmes on Ulster Television, he arrived covered in overcoats as usual and we tidied him up as best we could. The director of the programme had no idea of what a secret weapon I was unleashing upon him. The introduction over, there was RB talking at six-seven words a second, with the brain at double that pace and the programme was almost a monologue, but was very informative, educative and, somehow or other, he had included the third adjective of Lord Reith's adage about broadcasting – it was 'entertaining.' Almost by osmosis, he had adapted to the medium and was communicating with the largest 'lecture class' that he had ever encountered.

He came hotfoot to the Boardroom afterwards and I congratulated him on his performance, which he gracefully acknowledged. I then offered him a drink. One of his loves in that quarter was Port and he succeeded in demolishing a whole bottle in half an hour, without turning a hair. He then requested to see round the studio and what should have been a short trip turned into one that took several hours. He became fascinated by the equipment and quizzed all the engineers about what they did, how they did it and what was all the electronic gear. He found it totally fascinating and, as ever, absorbed everything. When he returned to the Boardroom for even more Port, he summarised the experience which he said was unique, by saying 'Somehow I wish I had a technical background.' Another Farraday?

DR BRUMWELL HENDERSON CBE (1954)

RELUCTANT COOK

RB invited Jammy Clinch to come to dinner one Friday. Clinch shifted Commons and repaired to the Junior Dean's rooms in the Rubrics. He was given two glasses of Claret before RB said '*You've come to dinner?*' Clinch agreed that this was so, whereupon RB disappeared into his pantry reappearing with a tin of digestive biscuits. '*This will do us!*' he said. Jammy, however, felt that this did not quite make up for missing Commons.

DR CHRISTOPHER PETIT (1954)

Another McDowell memory was being invited to "supper" at one of his clubs, and sitting there, listening to his stream of stuff, and wondering when the "supper" would appear. It turned out that "supper" consisted of a number of glasses of whiskey! I also remember him taking me to visit Marsh's Library, and, of course, many evenings in his hilariously unruly rooms, drinking rubbishy sherry.

DR RICHARD STACK (1962)

RELUCTANT HOST

Clive Murphy (1958) told me that McDowell maintained a house in North London for many years. As he was seldom there for extended spells, security was a problem. He said that a useful ploy was to leave some pound notes scattered about in conspicuous places – to deter intruders from delving deeper and finding more valuable items.

PETER IRONS (1966)

WELCOME GUEST

He became one of the most sought-after dinner guests in the country houses around Dublin, not to mention London.

ERIC WAUGH (1952)

THE HIST

*Founded in 1770, The College Historical Society
is the oldest of all university debating societies.*

RB McDowell in the Chair

A legendary orator, Dr McDowell's speech to the bi-centennial meeting of the Society is said to have been interrupted, by applause, forty-one times in one hour!

NIGHT ROLL

1958

The Junior Dean, Dr RB McDowell, escorted by a porter of the night watch, sets out to take 'Night Roll'.

The alleged origin of the Junior Dean being preceded by a porter with a lantern is that some students, for fun, once dug a trench on the normal route that the JD took. He fell in and, as a result, ordered the porters to carry a lantern so that this would not occur again.
SIMON WEBLEY (1957)

RB McDowell
I think that the lantern was lit. I think we can safely say, lit –
I have a vague memory of a gutting candle.

Last time we were at our summer-house on the Greek island of Aoba, RB came to stay with us. We had a spare room there with two little beds and Gina, my wife, took care to see that both beds were equally comfortable, arranging reading lamps and so on. RB demurred as to which bed to sleep in and then he made his choice. He slept in both.

ANTONY MARECCO

He was a most charming, kindly house guest and I particularly appreciated the way that, as he was departing, he sought out my son, Christopher, in order to wish him good luck in his forthcoming A Level examinations.

JANE WRIGHT (COOKE) (1966)

He first came to stay with us on a hot summer's day in July in, I believe, 1982. Due to the heat that day, I was wearing the minimum amount of clothing possible. He arrived in his overcoat, hat, scarf, suit (including waistcoat), sweater, shirt and another sweater underneath. He had his raincoat underneath his overcoat as it saved him carrying it! He had come by train from Oxford, having rung the previous night to invite himself to stay. Ann took the original phone call and, when he requested to speak to me, told him that I was not at home. He then said it was a private matter whereupon Ann informed him that she was my wife – at which he invited himself to stay! We are currently on our third generation of cocker spaniels, all of whom have been named after World War II commanders, i.e., Alexander of Tunis, and another currently is Tedder, a marshal of the RAF. 'Alex,' who is his favourite, enjoys RB's visits almost as much as we do. Alex is a scrounger and sits waiting for the frequent offerings that tend to drop off RB's side of the table.

He is coming for Christmas again. We believe it is his twenty-third year. I am afraid I have exchanged the Rolls – his preferred form of travel – for a recent model Bentley but it will be just as comfortable for him and I shall make arrangements to have an appropriate photograph of him taken during the Christmas period.

SIMON NEWMAN (1966)

11

Revolving Happenings

THE SHOOTING OF THE JUNIOR DEAN

1960s

In the world of Trinity, history repeated itself. Undergraduates, newly arrived in College, often discovered a good story from the distant past and would then decide to re-run it, as if they had just thought of it themselves. This is the background to the episode known as 'The Shooting of the Junior Dean' which goes as follows:

One evening, Dr McDowell enters Front Square – from the direction of Front Gate or the Dining Hall – depending on the narrator – when a shot rings out, several students walking nearby fall down pretending to be dead and a voice shouts from an upstairs window: 'You're next, McDowell! At this, the JD collapses or runs towards the Porters' Lodge crying 'Murder!' Those responsible are never caught.

I was aware of the event for I was in Botany Bay at the time. It was a 2.2 pellet for sure, fired from a top floor window.

PETER LAUB (1967)

I was not lucky enough to have witnessed gun-shots echoing across Front Square when the JD was one day meandering and muttering his way across this hallowed quadrangle, so I have to rely on my only source at the time and until her death in 1997. Rosemary Gibson was a great chum of Simon Morgan who had rooms in the GMB overlooking Front Square at the time of this incident.

Simon was the son of the Headmistress of Alexandra College (which Rosemary had attended briefly and sabotaged frequently). He was also a flamboyant dresser and party-giver whose functions were guarded by bouncers in battledress behind barbed-wire perimeter fences ... and guests had to pay to enter. Simon's abiding passion seemed to be firearms, of which he possessed several, presumably unlicensed in those wild days before 1969. Rumour had it that Simon the incorrigible exhibitionist was the one who fired the shot or shots from his perfectly positioned perch and who, observing the JD's undivided attention for that moment, shouted out in a Northern Irish accent words to the effect that McDowell was next ... knowing Simon, he probably used a megaphone, such was his love of gadgets and militaria.

ANDREW GIBB (1966)

Unbeknown to the perpetrators, however, none of this was new to RB McDowell!

TWENTY YEARS EARLIER

I entered Trinity in 1945. The Professor of Zoology had rooms on the top floor in New Square. He kept a shotgun there. He felt it safer than in his house in Wicklow. His two sons, Peter and David Bronte-Gatenby, lived in his rooms. You kept warm with bags of turf, no coal being available. One day, McDowell was chattering away in the hall, or on the steps, when one brother fired his father's gun. The other let go a bag of turf on the top landing. It rolled down a flight of stairs ending with a thud on the next landing. This was followed by 'You're next, McDowell!'

DR CHARLES HAYTHORNTHWAITE (1950)

AND SIXTY YEARS BEFORE THAT:

In 1880, George Wilkins, a Junior Fellow with a bad attitude, was appointed Junior Dean. He imposed new rules so unpopular that, within the week, enraged students were following him around College, brandishing guns, threatening to shoot. He was quickly replaced and order was restored.

OR WAS IT?

His successor, A. C. O'Sullivan, lasted for three weeks!

The next incumbent, M.W.F. Fry held on for five years – but only by lying low. It took him three years, according to an article in Punch, to dare to put up a note telling the students that they could no longer jump on top of the tables at Commons and run around shouting and fighting. Three years! Not indicative of a man who had much of a grip. RB McDowell would have sorted those characters out – in three minutes.

DEVOTIONS AT DAWN

In spite of all this, it was still thought that Trinity undergraduates were – more or less – 'gentlemen' but, as RB has pointed out, the term 'gentleman' in Ireland at that time merely indicated a person who did not have to get up in the morning should he not wish to do so. There being no shortage of candidates in this category, the tale of the 'Sun Worshipper' entered the annals of College.

This came about at a time when a student entering Trinity was required to declare his religion – any religion – and then to attend the church of his choice once a week, that is, on Sunday morning. This timing was, understandably, not always convenient, following as it did so closely upon Saturday night, and over the years a number of young 'gentlemen' declared themselves to be 'sun worshippers' a sect unencumbered with either church or clergy. The first recorded instance of this scam dates back to the beginning of the century, during the reign of 'the great Mahaffy.'

RB McDowell describes one of these occurrences in 'Mahaffy: A Biography of an Anglo-Irishman', co-written with Professor Stanford:

'When an undergraduate entered 'sun-worshipper' as his religious denomination in his matriculation form, on the first morning after he had slept in his college rooms, he was awakened at dawn by a loud knocking on his door. Opening it, he saw a college porter: 'Provost's compliments, Sir; it's time to say your prayers to the rising sun.' After some days of this he changed his religion.'

In the 1950s, RB himself is Junior Dean:

(Three accounts)

At dawn, after his first night in the Rubrics, the sun worshipper was awoken by a loud hammering on his door. It was the JD, who advised a dishevelled figure that his God was about to appear and he'd better look sharp about it.

ROB MERRICK (1965)

A student entering rooms for the first time completed a form where he wrote 'sun worshipper' in the section denoting religion. The story goes that the *JD did not let it pass* as youthful frivolity but every morning at sunrise got the said young man up out of his bed to worship the sun before the Campanile.

SANDRA WEST WANG (1968)

Enter the porters:

In the 50s, I and my twin brother resided in College rooms at No. 34, New Square. In No. 35 on the 3rd floor lived one George C------, a hopeful youth who wished one day to become a doctor. Both he and my brother were in the same Year and that is how I made his acquaintance.

In those days it was the custom of the Junior Dean to invite each new resident to his rooms for an informal chat, and to ensure he was at ease in his changed surroundings. George C-------- was duly invited. Here I must mention that George was an Englishman from an old landed Yorkshire Catholic family who never recognised the Reformation and had had a strict eye kept on his upbringing.

George was by character a youth of a stubborn nature, inclined to kick against the traces, so when the Junior Dean asked his religion, to advise him of his nearest place of worship, George stated that he had been a Catholic but had lately been converted to Sun Worship.

The JD mildly enquired which sect of sun worshippers he favoured, and reeled off a list of possibilities out of which George picked The Ancient and Venerable Order of the Oak (founded in 1901). The JD made a note of this and bade him good afternoon. This was on a Sunday. Later that evening/morning, George rolled into bed after a demanding few hours in Davy Byrne's with some thirsty mates. At 5a.m. he was dragged from a heavy slumber by a thunderous banging on his heavy oaken front door. George groped into his hallway and opened his door to reveal two college porters, members of the night watch, complete with a lantern.

'Yes?' enquired George.

'De Junior Dean presents his compliments, sor, an' requests dat youse get up an' worship de sun, sor,' was the reply.

They further informed him that they were obliged to witness his act of worship, which should last at least 10 minutes.

George led them both into his sitting room to open his curtains, and, while they stood and watched, began some mumbo-jumbo facing the eastern sky. However, in his fuddled state, his liturgy soon ran out of steam.

Now one of the porters was a part-time chorister at St Patrick's Cathedral and, anxious to show off his prowess, suggested that they should round off the proceedings with a hymn. George was by this time fully in agreement and the porter, who by all accounts had a very serviceable bellow, rendered:

> *'Che bella cosa na jurnata è sole,*
> *N'aria serena doppo na tempesta!*
> *Pe' ll'aria fresca pare già na festa...*
> *Che bella cosa na jurnata è sole'.*

etc. while George stood there half asleep holding up his pyjamas.

That was Monday morning. The ceremony was repeated the next morning, and the next. On the Thursday George called on the JD to inform him that he did not find sun worshipping spiritually satisfying and had decided to return to the religion of his fathers. '*A wise choice*,' said the JD dryly. '*Sun worshipping, I feel, has very little future in our country; especially with our climate.*'

VINCENT BYRNE (1956)

INTERCHANGEABLE TALES

MAHAFFY AND McDOWELL

RB defines the tale of the sun worshipper as 'another of those traditional stories that are passed on from one man of 'high position' and 'jocular disposition' to a successor.' It is a description that fits himself and Sir John Mahaffy, to perfection. To many people, the roles of these two Trinity giants and the tales that were endlessly repeated about them are interchangeable.

TWO EXAMPLES, BOTH UNTRUE:

The story goes that, on first arriving in College, the jocular person does not know many people. To cover up this social solecism, he stands outside his rooms of an evening calling loudly, (for example), 'Are you there, McDowell? Are you there?'

At the Shelbourne Hotel, one evening, a group of Trinity eminences, deep in discussion, are rudely interrupted by an inebriated person requesting directions to the cloakrooms. 'Follow the corridor until you see a sign marked 'Gentlemen,' the person of high position and jocular disposition replies, 'but do not let that deter you!'

13

Home & Abroad

JUXTA DUBLIN

It was through rambles with RB that I was first introduced to such landmarks of old Dublin as The Brazen Head pub and Marsh's Library. He also liked to visit places much further afield and after I acquired my first car, a rather dilapidated Ford Prefect, he would propose drives into the country. One of these was to Newgrange and other megalithic monuments in the Boyne valley. Another was to Hunter's Hotel near Ashford where we had tea. An excursion which ended less comfortably took place in the winter. We were driving towards Roundwood and though there had been quite a heavy snowfall the car seemed to be coping quite well with the conditions. So with the rashness of youth I ventured up a side road. The snow was much deeper there and we soon got stuck. Luckily there was a cottage nearby and I was able to borrow a shovel. As I dug and scraped away, RB stamped around trying to keep his circulation going. His habitual attire of hat, scarf and overcoat certainly proved its worth on that occasion!

SIR RIVERS CAREW BT (1956)

THE WEST

In a rare burst of generosity, my parents had given me, for TCD, a 1930 model Austin Seven, the same age as myself. This car was reliable, so far as its engine was concerned but the rear springs were constantly breaking. RB and I planned a tour of Connemara, but before this could happen something had to be done about the car's springs. I found a wooden wedge and, with a sledge-hammer, drove this home, between the broken spring and the chassis, so more or less levelling the car. Before setting off westward, there was a brief discussion as to who would pay for what. We agreed to split costs. I'd pay for petrol, if RB would do the same for engine oil. It was a little unfair as I was more or less certain that the car's appetite for costly engine oil equalled, if not exceeded, its demand for petrol, which was much cheaper. And so it proved – maybe a quart of oil to fifty miles. Where we went, in the West, and where we stayed, have long since been forgotten. The car never let us down, and RB was, as always, a delightful companion and never complained of the spring-less drive, over the bumpy and pot-holed Western roads.

DR PETER DEMPSTER (1952)

A SECRET MISSION

McDowell, accompanied by the Curator of the TCD Library, William Parke, took the Book of Kells to London for exhibition at, I believe, the British Museum.* The journey was made in great secrecy and to minimise the possibility of theft, they took the mail boat from Dublin dressed as impoverished Irish emigrants, which of course was no problem for McDowell! The Book of Kells itself was carried in a battered suitcase.

DR CLIVE WILLIAMS (1965)

* The British Museum had evidently been forgiven its duplicitous reluctance to return the Book of Kells to TCD after it was sent there for re-binding in the 1870s.

DR CLIVE WILLIAMS (1965)

GATES OF PARADISE

I recall one lecture, as a Freshman in the 1940s, in the Regent House above Front Gate, at which McDowell described his first visit to Florence (I think he travelled in a motorcycle sidecar). He was disconcerted to find he could not get near Ghiberti's sculpted bronze doors on the baptistery of the cathedral (dubbed by Michelangelo 'The Gates of Paradise') because of a scrum of American tourists. '*I trust*' said he, in a typical afterthought, '*that when I make my final approach to the gates, there will not be such a crush barring the way.*'

ERIC WAUGH (1952)

THE ADRIATIC

I knew him very well. Indeed, on one occasion we made a trip to Italy together. My parents lived in Geneva, and I would generally go home for the summer holidays. One year, I was with my father at the garage where he had his car serviced, when the owner showed us a 1938 Buick, an enormous and extremely fast car with running boards, which I bought for about $100. It was, needless to say, my pride and joy and I conceived, during the year of 1959, the notion of taking a summer trip around Northern Italy in it, and mentioned this to Dr McDowell. We arranged that he should accompany me, since he didn't drive himself and the cost of petrol for the big car was rather steep, and I thought it would be fun.

Accordingly, he got himself over to Geneva and we set off across the Alps for a couple of weeks, staying in Florence, Venice, Ravenna, and no doubt other places that I have forgotten. It was the first time that I had spent so much continuous time with Dr McDowell and I found I had to take certain measures. He was to sit in the back, and read or snooze. The talking could start again as soon as we arrived somewhere, but while driving, I tried, as tactfully as possible, to keep him quiet. It was an excellent arrangement, and we got on famously. I was delighted to have such a splendidly interesting companion on the trip.

I have a couple of fine anecdotes, notably the sight of the Junior Dean sitting on the beach in midsummer, somewhere near Ravenna, wearing his trademark outfit: hat, scarf, overcoat (talking non-stop, of course). I remember we visited Venice and I looked up a gondolier whom I had met during an earlier visit. RB and I spent the day in the gondola, visiting one bar after another, drinking weak Italian beer every twenty minutes or so. The quid pro quo was that he (the gondolier) got to drive my Buick around the Veneto, a remarkable thrill!

DR RICHARD STACK (1962)

PARIS IN THE SIXTIES

Quite inadvertently, McDowell came up against the student revolt in Paris in the late sixties and had no option but to follow the protesters into a large lecture hall where the French authorities were denounced in the roundest of terms. He reported later that, while having little sympathy with the views of the rebels, he had found the occasion a quite thrilling experience!

PROFESSOR TREVOR WEST (1960)

RB McDowell

Paris!

The thing I like about Paris is that one is not expected to be always spic and span!

A SQUARE IN CORINTH

One would think that the JD's appearance was unique, but in the summer of 1963, I had a strange experience in Greece. I was sitting with my girlfriend in an outdoor café in a square in Corinth when a man *looking exactly like him*, went by! Although my girlfriend was not a fellow student, she often came into College and was well familiar with the JD's appearance. When we saw this man pass the café, we both gaped at one another in astonishment and were so convinced he was the JD that we left our table and followed him round the square and into a neighbouring street. It was only when he disappeared into the police station that we wondered whether he was not the JD but the JD's Greek double!

PROFESSOR MARTIN SMITH (1962)

II ~ TRINITY IN THE GOLDEN ERA

14

Background

EARLY DAYS AT TRINITY

In 1592, when Trinity was founded, the Provost and Fellows were invited to choose 'Whatsoever laws they considered well constituted in the Universities of Cambridge or Oxford'; *but neither that first Board, nor any other Trinity Board, ever followed the Oxbridge model slavishly and Trinity was always different. As the centuries went by, relations with Oxford and Cambridge remained close and cordial but, just occasionally, a spat of one-upmanship would break out. For example, one of the others once dubbed Trinity the 'Silent' Sister', hinting at a (temporary) scarcity of publications. It was a preposterous sobriquet for a University boasting so many great names and sharp tongues and Trinity retaliated with two innovative coups of her own.*

DARING DECISIONS

The first of these occurred in 1793, when TCD admitted Catholics to degrees, long before Oxford even thought of it and sixty-seven years before she did anything about it. Then, in 1904, Trinity not only admitted women to degrees, but extended the arrangement ad eundum, *to ladies who, in spite of having passed their exams at Oxford or Cambridge, were still being deprived of the magic piece of paper by those universities. While the other 'sisters' dithered, seven hundred and fifty of their ladies arrived in Dublin to collect their degrees from Trinity – and a canny Board pocketed the fees, which were used, fittingly, to refurbish Trinity Hall. A. L.*

SCHOLARSHIPS

SCHOLARS

At the end of their second year, all undergraduates could sit for 'Schol', a competitive examination that rewarded the winners with a range of privileges including free commons, a reduction in fees and a seat on the University Board as 'Scholars of the House'.

But for some even this was not enough.

The porters at Front Gate were surprised one day when a Scholar turned up on a horse and insisted that he was entitled to have the animal fed and watered whilst he was taking an exam. The JD was informed. Dr McDowell checked Scholarship privileges, then went across to the Examination Hall, located the Scholar and fined him for being improperly dressed. He was not wearing the required sword!

ROB MERRICK (1965)

SIZARSHIPS

Given that, in those days, undergraduates – or their parents – had to pay their own fees, people who had the ability but not the money could apply for a 'Sizarship' – a College grant that was based on financial need as well as academic ability:

Although my father was a Sizar and a triple gold medallist as a scholar in Latin, Greek and Sanscrit from 1918-1922, he never fully explained to me what it was, as he was a very private sort of man. I understood that it was a special scholarship taken on entry to Trinity that included all fees paid, plus free commons; free (very basic) college accommodation and a very small monetary grant. My father was the youngest son in a family that included three daughters and an elder brother twenty years his senior, who went to Oxford. By the time my father went to Trinity there was no money. He told me that he used to buy a bag of potatoes at the beginning of each term that had to last him throughout the term on days when there were no Commons. I surmised that there was no gas or electricity in his rooms as he was very adept with kerosene 'primus heaters' and lamps. I guess there may have been a coal fire as he was very adept at, and preferred, to make toast by it. He was also extremely and painfully frugal especially in regard to shoes. He resurrected a rusty old bike which he used for commuting and for trips from Dublin to his parents' home near Londonderry during vacations or when he could afford the time.

HENRY KENNEDY-SKIPTON (1962)

RB McDowell
'Trinity in those days was a spartan, small,
but intellectually alive, world'.

THE GOLDEN ERA BEGINS

Some people say that the Golden Era started in 1946 when the ex-servicemen came back from the war, while others claim that it was 1956, the year when RB McDowell became Junior Dean, and that it ended when he relinquished the role in 1969. But no one knows for certain - for this is a mythical era created by fond, if distant, memories. Much depends on when you were there yourself! Regardless, however, of precise dates, the Era's grip on the emotions of those 'who were there' is very strong. Recently, when a Speaker, at a reunion in London, invited his listeners - of mature years, their undergraduate days, you would think, long forgotten - to imagine that they were nineteen again, standing at Front Gate, about to walk into Trinity for the first time - there was hardly a dry eye in the house.

A.L.

15

The Forties, Fifties & Sixties

It was the happiest time of my life. It was amazing that we got qualifications. Trinity still had an aura of pre-war Oxford or Cambridge. I think that it was rather a special period and it needs to be recorded.

RANDAL KINKEAD (1954)

The student body was a curious, happy mixture. Since the college was still officially 'banned' by the Roman Catholic Church, there were relatively few Irish Catholics among the 2,000 undergraduates. The Ulster continent made up about forty percent of the student body, and there were also many from England – Trinity was still a popular option for English school-leavers who would otherwise have gone to Oxford or Cambridge. Numerous British ex-servicemen, who arrived just after the War, brought an unusual experience of life (and death) to the place, and there were others even more exotic: a Polish prince, the scion of a French champagne family, several Lebanese and Egyptians and a group of sixty Nigerians. Women students made up a small, lively and welcome minority, though they were not allowed rooms in college and were carefully counted out at the gate at 6 p.m.

DR BRUMWELL HENDERSON CBE (1954)

SOCIAL LIFE

The gossip was as continuous and regulated as in the days of Addison and Steele. Like theirs, it was fed by reliably accurate witticisms in the Miscellany, cherishing the same dozen names easily recognised in spite of the substitution of dots for vowels. These celebrities wove their enchanted way among the visible minority to be seen criss-crossing Front Square, and were reported at every social event such as the Boat Club Do, Valerie's parties or Little-Go. The latter, for the benefit of younger readers, was a near-defunct oral examination in half-a-dozen subject areas claiming to bestow educational breadth on six years dominated by degree specialisms. Waiting one's turn in the Exam Hall, we met old friends, compared the number of re-sits achieved, and mourned those for whom some mathematical or scientific blockage had meant departure from college. For many, in fact, work was an unthreatening interruption to the main business of the social whirl, failure being attributed largely to preoccupation with politics, religion or sport. Only when one of the Legendary Ones clip-clopped out with sheepish disappointment, was an excessive social life suspected.

Predominantly, however, an often romantic but mainly platonic social life radiated from the dozens of clubs and societies who set up their stalls at Front Gate at the beginning of every academic year, from the daytime parties accelerating towards Trinity Week, from the cricket 'spectators' competing in sunlit finery and from the splendours of the regular formal dances. Before the arrival of jeans and unsmuggled condoms, those relatively respectable 'Doris Days' may seem corny, irresponsible and parasitic, but self-motivated hard work, as well as late-night philosophising, flourished in the same liberal milieu. Its underlying humanism and detachment was embodied by Professor W.G. Stanford who at the United Nations solemnly warned Communists that, if they did not mend their ways, they should be banned from every museum and gallery in Ireland. As well as, we presumed our beloved coffee-houses.

JOE GOY (1953)

In May 1966, I invited my girlfriend and future wife, Rosemary Gibson, to the Trinity Week Garden Party in the Provost's garden. As a card-carrying iconoclast and enemy of pomposity, Rosemary insisted on challenging protocol by wearing a black plastic bin-liner over her head and torso, with suitable holes for eyes and arms to aid navigation and histrionics. Rosemary had a good pair of legs and a rippling giggle, so the cognoscenti were quick to identify the mystery woman on my arm ... but not De Valera, who was reputed to be there.

As we left, we wove our way past the old Reading Room into Front Square only to encounter a bemused JD, dressed in his usual winter wardrobe in the heat of early summer. McDowell was uncharacteristically lost for words in grappling with the hooded apparition that was Rosemary Gibson, a mischievous female student who had teased him mercilessly but not malevolently for her entire four years in college. It is difficult enough for anyone to converse with an anonymous woman with her head and shoulders in a bag: after all, how does one make eye-contact? McDowell spluttered on, temporarily robbed of his famous volubility but itching inside to discover the secret of my companion.

With the JD attached spellbound to Rosemary's hip, we were shortly joined, somewhere between the Campanile and No. 23, by R.B.D. French who had become reacquainted with his erratic English student at her graduation in 1965. R.B.D. had whispered to Rosemary from his seat on the podium how nice it was finally to meet her after all her years of failing to attend his lectures. The moment R.B.D. shared his inner knowledge of the lady in the bag with the JD, McDowell's power of speech was magically restored to its usual prowess and he scorched off again across the cobbles.

ANDREW GIBB (1966)

SEX

EX-SERVICEMEN

I remember, in the Forties, arriving as a young school leaver among all those experienced ex-servicemen – hard drinkers and womanisers!

DEREK FIELDING (1952)

MEDICS

During the past year, the number of medical students involved in court cases has been startling. How many are constantly drinking, wenching, speeding and gambling!

TRINITY NEWS 18.2.54

AND OTHERS

Despite the supposed Beatles revolution I feel certain that a great deal more sexual activity was going on in early-fifties Trinity than I even imagined at the time. I can only offer subjective recollections of a shy only child sailing from post-war depression and austerity to a promised land of relative freedom and plenty. At the first breakfast table, with its extraordinary piles of pre-war fried food, I recall five excited young men comparing their recent innocent approaches at the previous evening's 'hop' at the Dixon hall. Later, from the flourishing community of daily gossip, I gleaned that it was the ex-National Service undergrads who were more likely to be actually copulating, though this rumour may often have seemed remote from the fondly-recalled progression of reading-room chat, coffee in Grafton Street, dalliance on the Green and a blanket on Killiney Hill.

I am confident that those two inseparable queens of the Miscellany, Joan Schellenberg and Iris Quinn, would not object to being recalled as the toast of college for their charm and insatiable notoriety. They contrasted with the dozens of extraordinarily beautiful Irish girls from remote convents who effortlessly stood out in a largely multinational community, but who took longer to make friends in the endless sherry parties in rooms and late-night suppers in flats. Meanwhile the witty dotted comments and poems reached their climax when, due to some prophetic electrical fault, the missing 'H' in the huge neon sign above the Irish Sweeps Office revealed, to a male-dominated society, the possible future of girls devoted neither to work or marriage.

Whether or not I lived those idyllic years in blissful ignorance, the Board had no illusions about the dangers of horsehair sofas and turf fires. Women for a time were required to be out of college before six o'clock, later nine, though how this affected the popular tradition of afternoon tea in rooms, and what might ensue, was never clear. A tale concerning moonlit rope-ladders was sometimes whispered – I would still love to know the truth of the matter.

Constraints on sexual activity were in many respects as 'pre-war' as the availability of bacon, eggs and stockings. Many new Freshmen, while technically teenagers, came armed from southern English public schools with a confident sense of male leadership, if not superiority, as if already groomed for the Bar or the House of Commons. Indeed I believe the latter owes its debating etiquette to the founders of the 'Hist', in whose lounge 'men only' could sit silently in waistcoats and ties, perusing the Financial Times or Irish Tatler and Sketch. Even in mixed clubs such as the Mod. Lang. Society, noted for its cream cakes, or the Gramophone Society, held in a chilly lecture-room (bring your own cushion), emotional or romantic topics were discussed with solemn restraint. 'Faster' socialising was enjoyed by the élites who either rowed, kicked or acted, or hung around those who did. The Madrigal Society reduced bawdy Tudor pub-songs to meticulous innocence. By contrast the Choral Society, though not without its social opportunities, rehearsed two or three *oratorios* per year, proclaiming the more spiritual aspects of love and heaven.

JOE GOY (1953)

McDowall was in office in the days when female students were supposed to be off-campus by the chastity hour of 6.30 pm. He was aided and abetted by the fearless Dean of Women Students, the draconian Miss Bramble (sister of Wilfrid, Steptoe's impersonator), the scourge of every hot-blooded and lascivious male member of college. Primed by the obliging attitude of red-nosed Larry, the skip for DUBC and R.B.D. French at No. 23, a well-endowed oarsman friend of mine prevailed upon Bob, the skip at No. 38 in New Square, to facilitate his nefarious sexual exploits. After all, by 1963 college skips were an endangered species whose numbers had dropped from twenty-seven to eleven, whose weekly wage was under £5 for a seven-day week and whose pension at seventy had remained elusive ... none had survived long enough to enjoy more than three months of it! Faced with the prospect of natural wastage and the consolation of an annual freebie to Punchestown Races, Bob was a willing confidant in enabling this nameless rower and his equally nameless consort to enjoy an entire week of carnal pleasure, interrupted only by Bob's daily visits to collect money for food and a handsome tip for silence from the offending doorstep.

A week later, a beaming but exhausted couple emerged blinking into the sunlight, and normal cleaning duties were resumed.

ANDREW GIBB (1966)

I often wonder if the JD was aware (of course he was) of the 'goings-on' directly above his rooms of Chuck Hirsch, Frank Pender and Tony Dunn. They ran a kind of commune in there. A woman was carried in, in a suitcase, and carried out in the morning.

BRIAN LEWIS (1964)

RELIGION

To an escapee from secular London, religion seemed to be everywhere. In the town, passers-by customarily acknowledged churches with a prayer or hold gesture; one election focused on the ethics of life-threatening childbirth. Young people appeared to be content with heavily-chaperoned parish ceilidhs, and college life, albeit largely hermetic, bent to the national mood. From my 'wife' Dr Michael Reedy, the founder of the Laurentian Society, the first officially permitted Catholic club in college, I was given to understand that, but for him, eternal damnation was a possibility for Catholics who merely came to Trinity, whatever they got up to. Meanwhile men moving into college rooms occupied them on condition they accepted Anglican chapel attendance as compulsory (or showed evidence of moral guidance from elsewhere).

More visible within college were the activities of the Evangelical Union, mostly northerners, who sidled up to their previously-discussed potential recruits with the give-away sally *"Halloo, thur! How's lafe, than?"* While no doubt admirable in their daily devotions and concern for fellow-students, they came in for gentle teasing from a community unperturbed by the moral dangers lurking in lipsticks, stockings, coffee and cinemas. Inevitably the Miscellany was quick to report any E.U. couples seen to be breaking ranks in an elegant corner of Bewley's or even a middle row of the splendiferous Metropole.

JOE GOY (1953)

16

Rooms

DÉCOR IN ROOMS

Home at College was 'rooms'. Rooms in No 9, Front Square were shared with Randal Kinkead, as my room-mate or 'wife'. Not that the accommodation was luxurious – my parents were horrified when they first saw the filthy wallpaper, peeling paint, the rotting timbers and, worst of all, clear evidence of rats. Our 'skip' or servant, Tracey made the beds, cleaned out the fire and emptied the slop buckets (though not necessarily in that order and usually without washing his hands at any stage). He had been in the Royal Navy and approved of me as an officer's son.

DR BRUMWELL HENDERSON CBE (1954)

We had a skip who had been in the Royal Navy. He was very impressed that Brum Henderson's father was a Commander and he brought us tea in the morning.

RANDAL KINKEAD (1954)

No. 15, Botany Bay remains for me one of the happiest of my 'mental' rooms. These were the rooms where, if anyone was coming to tea, we had to collect the fireplace from around the sitting room and stick it back into the appropriate holes. Eventually, the JD chucked us out as its 'being unfit for human habitation' and put us in Sam Beckett's old rooms in 40. Bit like a prison. We were very happy in the Bay – dirty, cosy and congenial. I think Walsh, the Agent, made him do so.

BRIAN LEWIS (1964)

HEATING IN ROOMS

One evening, I think it was during the winter of 1958/9, there was a knock on the door of my rooms, No. 36 LG (New Square). I think I was in conversation with Trevor West at the time. The occupant of rooms on the top floor called for assistance. He said there was a fire in one of the bedrooms. I grabbed my torch and Trevor and I dashed upstairs. In the bedroom, we found smoke pouring from the mattress. It promised to be a cold night and the owner had put his bedside lamp under the blankets to warm the bed. We unplugged the lamp and used a bucket to douse the smouldering mattress with water. However, the occupant became agitated. He thought we were being over enthusiastic, with the result that less water was applied than if we had had a free hand. We returned to my rooms congratulating ourselves on a job well done. Half an hour later, there was another knock on the door. This time no words were necessary. We could see and smell the smoke. Once again we dashed upstairs. The mattress had re-ignited and this time, was giving off serious quantities of thick smoke. The mattress was stuffed with horsehair and we had not soaked it enough on our previous visit. We took the mattress down the stairs and outside. For completeness, I sprinkled it with methanol (fuel for my model aero engine) and put a match to it – a very satisfactory conclusion.

COLIN WILSON (1959)

GUESTS IN ROOMS

One night, after a party, Eoin ('the Pope') O'Mahony, a legendary figure, needed a bed and I offered him the sofa in our rooms in Botany Bay and he stayed for several nights. It is some indication of his modesty and charm that, on one night when I had thoughtlessly slammed my door and locked him out, he did not kick the door as was the custom and try to wake me, until the skip came in at around 7 a.m. The skip told me later that he'd found the Pope fast asleep in his clothes on the bare boards of the landing outside our door because he was reluctant to make a nuisance of himself.

HENRY CLARK (1950)

Fifteen years later:

Eoin 'The Pope' O'Mahony, a legendary figure, used to sleep in our rooms behind the sofa, under a heap of coats and my 'wife', Paddy Rolleston, gave him twelve cups of tea in succession one evening. He used to tell the story, with relish of how he, a Knight of Malta or some other Papal thing, was standing in St Peter's Square waiting for the blessing, among a gaggle of nuns, when his braces broke. Strange chap – a bit like Judge Kelly who used to lurk in the graduates' room near Players.

BRIAN LEWIS (1964)

[What – sleeping clandestinely in rooms, under the JD's nose? Unbelievable. I wonder if McDowell knew this? Ed.]

The Pope used regularly to sleep 'rough' anywhere he could get. The JD knew this. The point is, you need to know that 'The Pope' would not toast the King at the 1930 Auditorial Supper of 'The Hist.' That would be the reason for the JD's animus against O'Mahony, as far as I can see.

BRIAN LEWIS (1964)

ATTITUDES TO WOMEN

At school, we were indoctrinated by the ideas of Miss Beale, who had said that girls should be educated in the subjects that their brothers learned and not taught merely elegant accomplishments such as playing the piano, singing and art. They advised me to go to TCD since it was said to be fully co-educational (although, at that time, girls were still not allowed in the Dining Hall or to live in College).

Twenty years after I had left Trinity, in the 1980s, I went as a mature student to Cambridge University to read English Literature. There, I was told, to my surprise, that Cambridge had been the first university to admit females to degrees! I pointed out that at TCD, I had lived in Trinity Hall which had been partly funded by those females who had passed their Cambridge exams but were not given a degree and that, to have their degree conferred, they had had to come over to Trinity. I noticed, even then, in the 1980s, that Cambridge was still resenting and resisting the presence of women; whereas at Trinity, in the 1960s, an attitude of acceptance and civilised politeness had been demonstrated by our Junior Dean, Dr McDowell, and his example was followed by the whole college. Of course, we were still supposed to be out by a certain hour each evening but no one seemed to mind that, very much and in any case, there were ways of getting round this inconvenient dictum.

JILL MCEVEDY (1961)

Was this one of them?
In the spring of 1962 it was reported to the Junior Dean that one of the students, from the rooms with the tall ceilings in Botany Bay, had constructed a platform dais on a timber scaffold which was some ten feet above the floor, thus making it quite impossible for the skip or cleaners to get anywhere near his bed. Initially the Junior Dean seemed quite unperturbed at this innocuous eccentricity provided that no structural damage was done to College property. However, due to continued pressure and innuendo from the college servants he eventually demanded a direct explanation concerning the student's sleeping arrangements. The response was given that said student had only recently acquired his Private Pilot's Aviation Licence and that this had been achieved despite the fact that he suffered from occasional bouts of vertigo, however he had been advised that by sleeping at a stimulating distance from the floor he would subconsciously overcome his fear of heights and in the fullness of time could aspire to obtain a Commercial Pilot's Aviation Licence. The Junior Dean was much impressed at the young man's resolve and dedication to his future career and having apologised with good grace for any intrusion or misunderstanding that may have occurred, he admonished the skip for listening to gossip. There then followed, by common consent, a truce between all parties concerned until the arrival of Kim Novak, Laurence Harvey, and all the troupe from Metro-Goldwyn-Mayer but that's another story.

MARTIN P. J. BYRNE (1963)

RB McDowell
'*I don't mind a man who is drunk and who has women in his rooms so long as he doesn't let off fireworks!*'

GUNS IN ROOMS

In 1943, Peter Gleeson and his friend Gillespie decided that Italy's unconditional surrender called for celebration. Gillespie was very interested in guns and had a small arsenal in College. They agreed that a 21 gun salute would be appropriate. The celebration took place in Peter's rooms in Botany Bay. Two radios were set up on the outside of one of the windows, tuned to a UK channel. As the radios blared 'God Save the King,' the 21 gun salute began with the discharge of a double barrelled shotgun followed by various black powder muzzle loaders. They must have had a very good idea that they were stirring things up. Soon the place was swarming with porters. However, everything was quickly concealed, the perpetrators were not detected and no punishment followed.

COLIN WILSON (1959)

Here's one that was going around when I arrived. Bonar Law was supposed to sit in his rooms naked. One day the skip was bringing his breakfast up the stairs to his rooms, when the door suddenly opened and a naked AB-L shot a rat on the stairs with an air gun. The skip dropped the breakfast with the words 'Mary Mother of God! I never saw anyting loik dat since der Troubles.'

BRIAN LEWIS (1964)

From AB-L

As far as I can remember I don't think there is any glimmer of truth in the tale. I don't think I was in the habit of sitting naked in my rooms and I never had an air gun. The nearest approach to such barbaric behaviour against the wildlife of the College was fishing for cats with a kipper from the top of the Bay. The cats used to come out of the air vents or whatever of the Bay cellars. I had a 9mm Luger, if that is any good, but I never shot no rat with it.

THE HON. ANDREW BONAR LAW (1959)

ANIMALS IN ROOMS

The Rat

One afternoon, I was having tea with a chap called Hedley, in his rooms, when I became aware we were not alone. A large black rat had me in his gaze. When I mentioned this, Hedley said 'He often comes up here from the docks.'

BRIAN LEWIS (1964)

The Donkey: Version One

Bill Smyth (1950 or thereabouts) described this incident to me several years ago. It must have occurred in the late 1940s. At that time a donkey was used to pull the mower that cut the grass in College Park. One day, some Engineers took the donkey and managed to persuade it into the Museum Building and up the stairs to the Engineering School. Once there, however, the donkey refused to go back down the stairs. All efforts having failed, a block and tackle was rigged up outside a window and the unfortunate animal was lowered to the ground. I didn't think to ask how they managed to get it to go through the window.

COLIN WILSON (1959)

The Donkey: Version Two

One summer evening after Commons, Huet Wilson, Bob Lumley and A.N.Other were strolling in College Park when they found a donkey, and having noticed a builders' hoist outside the Engineering Building where works were in progress, decided to bring the donkey into New Square and put it on the hoist. They then lifted it up and pushed it through a first-floor window where it stayed, outside the office of the then Junior Dean, Frank Mitchell, who found it next morning surrounded by a heap of donkey excreta.

PETER TICHER (1947)

SPORT IN ROOMS

Somebody, I think it was Ronnie Wathan, used to stand in rooms, probably No. 15, on the second floor, with the window open, and drive a golf ball down D'Olier Street! Good thing this did not come to RB McD's attention.

DR KEITH FERGUSON OBE (1964) as told him by DR MICHAEL HAYES (1955)

PORT IN ROOMS

The drinking of port was a cherished tradition in all the old universities. In 'Decline and Fall', set at Oxford in the 1920s, for example, Evelyn Waugh describes members of the Senior Common Room watching, delighted, while the super-rich members of the Bollinger Club leave a trail of destruction. The fines, to be imposed (by themselves) the following morning, should be sufficient, they calculate, to furnish the Senior Common Room with 'A whole of year of Founder's Port!' But, at TCD, things were – as ever – done differently. There, on at least one occasion, it was the Senior Common Room which, inadvertently, provided port for the undergraduates:

I'm sure it was George Wingfield, who said on Commons one night concerning the Senior Common Room 'They keep decanters of port out, up there, and I'm going to have some of it' There was scaffolding against the windows, so he climbed up the scaffolding, went in through the window, drank the port, but on his return, fell off the scaffolding and broke his arm.'

BRIAN LEWIS (1964)

George Wingfield replies:

Well! Brian Lewis's story about me and the port does, I concede, contain a grain (or perhaps a grape) of truth but it presents a very incomplete picture. I did have a bit of a yearning for port in those days and I did set my sights on that which was left out in the Senior Common Room. So, one night, at a late hour, I went up with two colleagues to visit the aforesaid Common Room where a few professors were snoring away sonorously. Subsequently, we gave a very splendid party, to which we invited the JD and some of those denizens of the Senior Common Room. As you can imagine, the quality of the wines served by mere undergraduates caused some amazement – and later on, a certain amount of upset. In the long run I was struck down by acute gout at the early age of thirty-four and have never been able to enjoy port since without running the risk of serious pain due to this gout. As for falling off scaffolding and breaking my arm, I'm glad to say that is a complete fiction.

GEORGE WINGFIELD (1966)

The place was like nowhere else one knows or could even imagine! If GW did not fall off the scaffolding then who did? I cannot see how I could have invented the GW tale since it is so incredible. Grape of truth … !

BRIAN LEWIS (1964)

'TCD – A College Miscellany,' in those days, was written anonymously by people co-opted to be 'shareholders', and to drink its then quite decent dinners, of which the best, probably at the end of Hilary term, after the Valentine's number, was always then held at the late lamented Louis Jammet's restaurant on Dame St, opposite Fellows' Garden. Some dons were regular (and very willing) invitees: R.B.D. French was one, McDowell another, David Webb, the botanist, a third. There would be three or four, absurdly good, wines – not to mention the fare. After one of these dinners, McD selected me to be taken back to his Front Square rooms for more port and conversation. I was already fairly speechless by the time we set off, back across the Fellows' Garden and Front Square, and have only the sense of a continuous high-pitched buzzing noise before sinking into a deep sleep. I've no idea how I got back to my rooms in Botany Bay.

W. L. (BILL) WEBB (1953)

RB McDowell
Port!
The most fatal of drinks – if you take too much.

BODIES IN THE BAY

THE DEER FROM POWERSCOURT

The year is 1954

You may remember an American Hollywood actor, one William Bendix; I saw him once beat Alan Ladd to a pulp in some gangster epic or another. Terry was his younger version: vastly overweight, arms like my legs, hands like bunches of bananas, very little neck, an oversized head with a mat of tight flaxen curls, large round baby-blue optimistic eyes and a mouth far too small for the rest of his face. He was second generation Irish, his father being a doctor in Liverpool. Terry was therefore a medical student and roomed in Botany Bay with two quiet English students who lived in terror of his mood swings, as indeed did his skip.

Terry was not much impressed by his flat mates but they had one redeeming feature: a car, which he was in the habit of commandeering from time to time for 'spins'. One Saturday, Terry decided he would like a 'spin' out to Powerscourt. On arrival Terry plunged into the surrounding woodland with glad cries and almost immediately started a fallow deer from the undergrowth. He returned shortly afterwards, dragging the now dead deer which he had killed, apparently, with his bare hands and which he was now bungling into the back seat of the car.

On the following Sunday morning in my flat on the top floor of 34 New Square, Sean, a mate of mine, interrupted my shaving. 'Come round to Terry's and see what he has in his bedroom,' he said. The mind boggled, but my wildest imaginings were outstripped by the sight of Terry himself kneeling on the bare floorboards of his bedroom beside a flaring gas ring and the corpse of the deer, which lay on its side with an aloof, bored look in its glassy eyes. Terry looked up and greeted me effusively from his kneeling position. I saw that he was wielding a large frying-pan. 'Hello there, Vince! Are you coming to me stag-party this evening?'

I did not reply as I backed out to the comparatively fresh atmosphere of the landing, where I released my pent up breath explosively, like a swimmer breaking the surface, and then fled down the stone stairs to the open air. I never went there again. The two English students left very shortly afterwards in a state of shock and Terry was left to enjoy his rooms in solitude. His skip, a respectable family man, was unwilling to report him to the Junior Dean.

Later, it was rumoured that on moonlit nights in Botany Bay, a stag's head could be seen framed in the window of Terry's rooms on the top floor – but I put that down to a trick of the light. This is gospel.
VINCENT BYRNE (1956)

THE DEER IN PHOENIX PARK, 1920s

I heard from the man concerned, who would have been in College in the Twenties, that he managed to kill a deer in Phoenix Park, bring it in, and hang it up in his rooms in Botany Bay. There were three or four people involved. In any case, the deer was hung up in the sitting room in Botany Bay and when the skip came in, in the morning, and saw a body hanging, he collapsed, thinking it was a suicide. I heard that from one of the people who killed the deer.

DR RB MCDOWELL

17

Dramatis Personae

LECTURERS

THE FRENCH DEPARTMENT

DR OWEN SHEEHY SKEFFINGTON

'Skeff' was ahead of his time. Faced with a mixed bag of Junior Freshmen, of divergent levels of fluency in the French language – meaning there were native speakers side by side with people straight from school – he took pre-emptive measures. First, he devised a cunning passage entitled 'Bonsoir Jacques' *reputed to contain every vowel and consonant in the French language and designed, like a dentist's drill, to weed out all impurities. Then, armed with a tape recorder, (a novelty in those days) he obliged everyone to record their version of the* opus *and listen to the replay. People were not so used, in those days, to hearing their own voice on tape, certainly not in public and, for many, it was quite a shock – especially when it was announced that the procedure was to be repeated at the end of the academic year when the improvement or otherwise could be judged. My own dismay was such that I left straightaway for Paris spending the next few months, if not always at the Sorbonne, at least on the* 'Boul-Mich' *– but in any case speaking no word of English. I returned in time for the replay. Later, I heard that Skeff had gone on playing my before & after versions for years, exhorting future intakes to note* 'what can be done!' *In my case anyway, his shock tactics had worked.*

A.L.

I'm interested in your account of my father's use of recorded sound, long before the language laboratory came to Trinity. His use of it went back long before 1960, as I remember his having a recording machine as long ago as 1949, but then it recorded, not on tape, but on steel wire. I well remember hearing "Bonsoir Jacques" many times on wires that I found subsequently and played on the machine to see what was on them!

DR FRANCIS SHEEHY SKEFFINGTON (1967)

Dr Owen Sheehy Skeffington was a dynamo of a personality who almost grilled you through the third degree in doing set piece translations. One would not have dared go unprepared to his class. The dividend came when we breezed through the dreaded Little-go, now mercifully abolished, when many others faltered.

DR JOHN CONNOR (1958)

MISS NORTH

In 1988, it was pointed out to me, by the Canadian Studies representative from TCD's French Department, that Miss Meta Evelyn North (1920) had been the subject of gross administrative abuse in that she had spent the whole of her career as a temporary lecturer. My response was that if there had been an effort to dispose of her in the 50s, there would have been a student riot that would have made 'soixante-huit' look like a picnic. Her lectures were relaxed explanations of grammatical structures and gentle efforts to get the pronunciations right. No small task when she had a significant enrolment from the Rugby and Boat Clubs, because the lectures were held at an hour which did not conflict with training sessions. She wore a mortar board and *pince nez*, neither of which I have ever seen since in the working environment. The exercise was carried out with charm and humour so much so, that she rated a quote a week in the College Miscellany.

DR JOHN CONNOR (1958)

THE ENGLISH DEPARTMENT

PROFESSOR WHITE

In the English Department we had to deal with Professor H.O. White, an antique specimen whose main claim to fame was his possession of an Elizabethan mouse-trap. He had very strict ideas about students wearing gowns to lectures, and about taking attendance. He was also quite ASTONISHINGLY boring! Put all these together, and you have the perfect strategy: come in without a gown, sit right at the front, on the left-hand side, where he started off the attendance register, sign it, and then, almost immediately, get thrown out for academic nakedness! Alternatively, sit at the back of the class, wait for the register to come around, sign it with various hands, using an assortment of pens for all your friends who were still in bed, and then climb out the window and head for the coffee shop.

DR RICHARD STACK (1962)

THE HISTORY SCHOOL c. 1950

RB McDOWELL, a brilliant & original thinker, whose lectures were delivered at machine-gun speed was, almost, in my generation's view, the 'Court Jester' to the magisterial, but shy, THEO MOODY whose fellow lecturers in the History School were the, apparently, disorganized but extremely wise, CONSTANTIA MAXWELL (Economic History); JOCELYN OTWAY-RUTVEN who was dry and assiduous and looked like an 18th Century Regency Buck (Constitutional History); and the charming ex-RAF English BASIL CHUBB, who was vaguely socialist and lectured us in Political History. A fairly good poker hand, with McDowell as the joker.

From 'Brum A Life in Television,' by DR BRUMWELL HENDERSON CBE (1954)

THE BURSAR

My initials are TCD and for four years every time I paid my fees, Captain Shaw would ask for my name and then my initials and when I said 'TCD' he would look up and say "Really?"

CHARLES MULRAINE (1962)

THE PROVOST
We had to bow to him, if living in College, when he passed.
I bet they don't do that any more.
BRIAN LEWIS (1964

THE PORTERS

Given that I was son, grandson and great-nephew of clergymen, it was not altogether surprising that the Divinity School thought (how wrongly!) that I might be a prospect. Which is probably why I was invited to tea one Sunday in November at Canon Dick Hartford's house. I set off on the bike for Rathgar. I got as far as the Front Gate, when Harry Hanson the porter said it was a very cold day to be cycling. He invited me into the snug at the back of the Porters' Box, where without great difficulty he persuaded me to have a slug from an unlabelled bottle, of *Poitin* as it happened. I headed off safe in the knowledge that there would be no alcoholic smell on my breath.

I returned from a very pleasant meal, after dark, and unscathed in terms of any risk of Ordination to find Harry in a state of great agitation. He'd given some of the beverage to his colleague on duty, Tommy Maher. Tommy, who had apparently been through the Burma or some such campaign and had contracted residual malaria, had promptly gone blind. I was asked if I could possibly put him up for the night on my sofa in the Rubrics. If I would leave my door open, they would fetch him out at 6 a.m. and bundle him into a taxi for home. If Dr McDowell were to enquire in the meantime, they would say that he was patrolling somewhere down the back end of College Park. A prostrate and, temporarily blind, Tommy, was duly stretchered to my room, and was gone by morn. From then on, I could do no wrong by the Porters!

J.W. (BILL) JACKSON (1961)

While on the subject of porters, I remember them really adding to the scene in Trinity in their brass-buttoned tailcoats and their hunting caps. They looked like *something* then. They were the JD's storm troops in the maintenance of discipline. Sometime in the interim, possibly in the early Eighties they were given the option of remaining in their traditional uniform as porters or going into a more modern dress and becoming 'Security.' Whether from bad taste or bad judgement, they opted for the latter; and so we see them today.

It's a little sad that when they obviously think they have improved their lot and their appearance, they should look more like porters than ever – only not porters on a gate (from *porta: a gate)* but railway porters (from *portare*: to carry. When one of the old porters approached you over something, possibly a message from the powers – that is, the JD – you gave respect to the uniform if not the man and took notice. Surely for ceremonial occasions it would not be asking too much of a security man to don the traditional porter's uniform if only, and quite literally, for appearance's sake.

MICHAEL BRERETON (1961)

I used to loiter in the Porters' Lodge for a chat on a quiet evening but I never knew their names. They did not wear the ubiquitous security badges of today. A medical student always gets burdened by the conversationalist's mother's asthma, hip, heart, stroke, or some foible of the missis. 'The Missis'. Of course, I was 'Sir' and respect was shown which excluded using their own names. 'Sir' was pronounced 'Sor'.

DR ADRIAN YOUELL (1968)

Andrew Bonar Law and I both played hockey, he rather better than me. We were studying the Hockey Club notice board together, to see if and where we would be required the following Saturday. Suddenly I was conscious that two men of gorilla proportions, quite obviously plain clothes Gardaí, were seeking to enter Front Gate and were totally blocking such light as came in that small entrance. They half-turned to the Porters' Box and were met by Arthur Unwin

– if you remember, a fine looking white-haired ex-soldier with matching moustache. 'We're looking for a Mr. Bonar Law,' they said. Arthur drew himself up to his full six feet, gripped both lapels with his thumbs and surveyed everyone in the Front Gate concourse, including – quite clearly – Andrew. 'Gentlemen,' he said, 'Mr Bonar Law does be a very hard man to find.'

J.W. (BILL) JACKSON (1961)

From AB-L

As usual I feel that there is a memory fault for I cannot recall such an event at Front Gate. Perhaps the conversation took place, but I wasn't there or if I was, I was blissfully unaware. What makes me doubt Bill Jackson's tale is that it was clearly daylight. Surely the front gates were opened fully in those days? However, there is perhaps some substance in what he says. The Guards did come looking for me once, accompanied by a short fat porter whose nickname was 'Malan' after the SA gentleman. He actually cornered me, cowering at the side of the catalogues in the semi basement of the Reading Room and when I asked him to say he couldn't find me – which he agreed to do, – his response was that I really should come out as they would get me in the end, which in fact they never did although it wasn't for lack of trying. They staked out our pad in Clontarf in a squad car for the best part of a week, which was a terrible nuisance. I had to get the bus back, go past the house and climb in over the back gardens. And then keep lights down and curtains drawn. Why the guards were looking for me is another story and related to an assist at the Pearse Street Gate given to me by the porter there.

THE HON. ANDREW BONAR LAW (1959)

The 'Bluebottle' was the porter whose job it was to announce the name of the Scholar who was to call Grace in Commons. He was also the College postman and knew all the students' names. He kept a book at Front Gate and when he saw people, he would stop them and say 'There's a letter for you.'

CHARLIE WEBB (COLLEGE PORTER 1956 – 1998)

This story was not witnessed by myself but was well known when I was at TCD 1958-62. You may remember a member of the staff, oldish chap in a cap who used to ride around the quad on a bike and was, believe it or not, responsible for security. He was known as "Homo Sapiens". The story has it that one night he was accosted in New Square by the JD, to whom he reported, and was told to come to the JD's office the following morning and collect his papers because he was being sacked for not doing his job properly. Homo Sapiens touched his forehead saying "Yes, Sir" and rode on his way a broken man. The next morning he went to the JD's office. The JD had no idea what he was talking about and told him to continue his duties. The Junior Dean who had accosted him the night before was Terry Brady in disguise.

CHARLES MULRAINE (1962)

EXTRACT FROM THE DIARY OF A COLLEGE PORTER:
Found two undergraduates attempting to light a An Tóstal candle on top of the Campanile at 3.07 a.m. In response to a request for names, gave Aldous Huxley and R.B. McDowell. Discovered on return to Front Gate there are no such names in Universal Calendar. Inexcusable blunder. Cannot remember similar blunder since Trinity Wednesday of '37. Fear am losing grip.

TRINITY NEWS, 20.5.54

THE GARDAÍ

Even the Gardaí seemed to think they came under the command of the JD. It was well known that, as soon as they saw him coming, they would all stop the traffic so that he could step straight into the street without having to look where he was going.

The Gardaí outside Front Gate stopping the traffic for the JD – true, this one, because I was there! Then, one night in the Stag's Head, Mike Cumming, Mike Newcome, Paddy Rolleston and some others and I did the following. We carried Kelvin Redford prone on our shoulders as if he had died/passed out, towards the

Gardaí. Whereupon he stopped the traffic for this 'emergency' to cross and then we swiftly put Redford down on the other side and all ran into Front Gate. There was a bit of trouble about this, I seem to remember. Then, years later, when we were staying at the Shelbourne, I ran into Father Sean Quigley who told us the strange story of Professor Stanford's funeral. He and the JD had decided to go to the funeral together and the JD said that it must be at St Michan's, because the Stanford vault (Sir C.V. Stanford etc) are/is all there. When they arrived, no funeral. So Quigley, being a priest, stopped a passing Gardaí car and said he needed to be at a funeral in Dalkey a.s.a.p. and they both got a lift to the real funeral.

BRIAN LEWIS (1964)

It was generally believed that, once past the Porters' Lodge, the Gardaí's jurisdiction ceased and the Porters, under the command of the Junior Dean, ruled.

RB McDowell

There was a vague tradition that the College was exempt from normal police action. But in fact, I don't think there is any basis in this. I remember, on one occasion at least, the police coming in when a policeman's cap had been stolen. The sergeant and a young constable met me and I identified the rooms – where the cap was recovered. The young constable was anxious for a charge but the Sergeant was less keen so it blew over. It would be difficult to find a legal base for the claim of immunity.

THE GARDAÍ AND THE ROPES

The year is 1959

The story so far: Joe Xuereb and Mike Brereton are giving a party at their flat in central Dublin. Dr Jim O'Brien, Brian Fisher and Tom Molyneux decide to gatecrash, (by rope), but unfortunately fall through a roof, smashing the glass and attracting the attention of the Gardaí who think it is an attempt on the British Embassy. The

Guards arrive to arrest everybody but instead stay to tea. Michael Brereton takes up the tale:

A certain irony in Dr Jim O'Brien's quoting Rushdie on the falsity of memory, for his report of the roof top arrest of himself, Brian Fisher and Tom Molyneux is a good example of what time and a fondly indulgent view of one's youthful scrapes and follies can do to a story.

I shared the flat with Joe Xuereb at the time and we were passing what was for us in those days a rarity, a quiet evening in – though not for long. There may have been two others with us that evening, but there was certainly no party going on when the Guards arrived (or it wouldn't have been tea we all ended up drinking). The party was somewhere else, never properly identified.

The flat was at 15 Hume Street, off Stephen's Green, and nowhere near the British Embassy. So there was no ring of steel round the whole block, and it was burglars and not terrorists the Gardaí fancied themselves in pursuit of – and with Brian Fisher in evening dress or natty dark suit and one of his inevitable brocade waistcoats, they must have thought they'd got Raffles at last.

And there were no ropes, nor was a searchlight shone from our back window: the Guards had to climb into our bath and from there onto the windowsill, and then lower themselves to make the short drop onto the floor of the valley below it before clambering up the next roof and into the night. There was some delay, and then they returned having apprehended their quarry. At least one Guard remained behind to assist in hauling them up again *as there were no ropes*. I am particularly confident that I recall these events accurately as I was very conscious at the time that, thanks to Joe's profligacy with his cast-offs, the valley floor was littered with a number of used condoms which I was not anxious to have traced back to the importer. Thankfully, the Guards did not look too carefully where they were putting their feet.

Other than that, Dr Jim's account rings pretty true, and the picture of miscreants, disturbed residents and officers of the law all sitting and standing around chatting and drinking tea and generally having a good old laugh about it all typifies the Ireland of that time – at any rate to my fond and no doubt, distorted, memory. As Dr O'Brien rightly surmises, the incident did not in any way involve the JD. One might add: fortunately.

MICHAEL BRERETON (1961)

[So – which true version is it? Ed]'

Mike Brereton's account of events I don't for one moment dispute – I myself have a vague memory of his description of them, but the story I sent you is not in any way related, neither is Heather O'Brien's. I did share a flat with Mike, but I also lived in other flats In Dublin. The story you published in *The Junior Dean* happened in my last year at Trinity when I moved into college rooms. My college rooms were in Front Square, on the top floor, and on the same staircase as the Junior Dean who was on the ground floor. Mike and Heather O'Brien's accounts should not be seen as contradictory as they happened in different places at different times. Happy days!

JOSE XUEREB (1963)

RB passing the Campanile c. 1966
© Chris Johnston

18

Extra Mural Pursuits

THE STUDY OF ALCOHOL

I did often wonder why ours was a four-year course as compared to everyone else's three year stint – until a fellow student told me the reason. The first year was not for academic studies but for the Study of Alcohol – of what to drink, how to drink it and finally how to hold it. Once you'd learned those skills, you were ready to academically rock.

TERENCE BRADY (1961)

'CLASSROOMS'

BARTLEY DUNN'S. This was a rather louche pub behind the Royal College of Surgeons. A lot of sailors went to it. I went a few times and was astonished by all the boating paraphernalia around the place. Staying at the Shelbourne two or three years ago, I asked about it and the porter told me it had been destroyed by the 'bandit Haughey' as Mrs Denard described him to us. The Denards salvaged the wonderful copper cauldrons during the dining room fire, from which we used to have our Commons served. They have preserved them at their house in Shankill since, otherwise, the cauldrons would have been chucked into the skip. They were used, I was told, by Oliver Goldsmith, when he was a Sizar, to bring up the food 'for his betters!'

We went to the BRAZEN HEAD occasionally and Brendan Behan used to 'hold court' there. He called me the 'bloody Eeenglish' one night in response to a perfectly reasonable question I asked him about Robert Emmett at whose table he was sitting. A repulsive man. Paddy Rolleston had a fascination with such people because his grandfather, T.W. Rolleston, friend of Yeats, had promoted them. We saw them through rose-tinted spectacles.

And I often think of trips to JAMMET'S to try to overhear what Dr Leventhal was saying to the ladies he was entertaining, or to listen to what I later found out was known as 'The Craik' (have I the correct spelling?) in the Shelbourne or to make evening visits to Bartley Dunn's or the Stag's Head.

BRIAN LEWIS (1964)

I remember an evening in one of the pubs when I was nobbled for another pint by a gentleman paddy who kept the conversation going with respectful 'Sors'. 'I passed through Thrinity meself sor, do ye credit dat. I walked in the front gate and out the back.'

DR ADRIEN YOUELL (1968)

At one time, I was living in a singing pub, well known to Joyceans, the BRAZEN HEAD, down in the mediaeval part of the city, said to be the oldest inn in Ireland. Since it was an 'inn' rather than a plain pub, it could stay open all hours and attracted a bohemian crowd late into the night, singing around the piano or to an old banjo.

One of the regulars was Brendan Behan. He was a notorious drunk; he was also a great scholar of Irish. Once, when he had been arrested in Bray for drunken behaviour, he insisted in court on all the proceedings, including the testimony of the policeman who had arrested him, being conducted in Gaelic (at that time, all civil servants, including the police, had to pass some sort of rudimentary exam in the language.) Naturally, the charges were dropped.

I remember meeting him once, on the Boulevard St Michel in Paris, when I was staying in the most revolting kind of "hotel" imaginable, somewhere on the Left Bank. The previous evening I (we, presumably?) had seen him, atrociously drunk, on stage at the theatre, where he had attempted to take off his trousers during his post-performance appearance! Such splendid times!

DR RICHARD STACK (1962)

THE BOAT CLUB

I was lured into the Boat Club by fantastic tales. It was stated that splendid entertainments took place when they went to country regattas like Fermoy and Limerick. In the words of the song, they said that one would find there *'cigareets and whisky and wild, wild women.'* Needless to say, rowing, was also, of course, reputed to be a healthy, manly sport, eight men in unison, steered by a midget cox. I soon found that there was another side to things, during training. No cinemas, theatres, smoking, and no large gatherings, 'For fear' our coach, Robin said 'for fear of infection.' I never knew whether he meant the common cold or some deadlier germ. Another rule was that we must take a pint of Guinness, no more and no less, each day, for our health. The Widow's pub at Islandbridge was recommended, for quality and price.

I started by rowing stroke, setting the pace and face to face with Roger, our cox, a delightful small-sized County Clare man. His main job was to steer our craft and urge us on, with cries of 'We're coming up on them – give her ten.' This meant ten Herculean strokes, the very oars flexing. I never really took to rowing. Comradeship, certainly. Enjoyment, when actually racing, minimal. Severe pain, yes. Quite soon, Robin, our coach, moved me to the bow of the boat where no one would have to follow my dithering pace. One winter's day we took part in a 'friendly' race. We rowed slowly – 'paddling' they called it – to the start. Our opponents were ready and the race went off in the usual way, massive efforts to get best position in the first four hundred yards and so take the quickest course around the bend. We failed in this. A quick glance over my shoulder showed that our rivals were leading by at least two boat-lengths.

Roger began his loud and untrue cries of 'You're coming up – only a length now, lads.' Our stroke upped the pace and I began to suffer, in the familiar way. Cramps in the stomach, griping pain in both shoulders and arms. But worse of all was the fear that my wrists would seize up and I would be unable to handle my oar properly. Thus I might 'catch a crab,' the oar at the wrong angle, plunging deep into the water. To this day I believe that 'a crab' in a racing eight would mean that one would be forced to let go the oar, to one's eternal shame. In any event, we lost the race. I caught no 'crab,' but was racked with pain and completely exhausted. We manoeuvred the boat to the pontoon, in front of the boathouse. Our coach Robin was there, having followed us down the towpath, on his bike. 'Next time, Peter, try!'

DR PETER DEMPSTER (1952)

TRADITIONS AT COMMENCEMENTS

Immediately after Commencements, it was traditional for third year engineers to capture one or more of the new graduate engineers, frog-march them up to St Stephen's Green and throw them into the lake. Fellow engineer, David English, and I made careful plans to avoid this ignominy. When the ceremony was over, we waited until everybody had left the Examination Hall and then climbed out through a window at the back of the stage. That the window could be opened easily had been checked out beforehand. We sprinted across the grass to the railings along Nassau Street and started to climb. It was exactly at this point that we were captured. Unfortunately, our plan had been rumbled. We were taken out through Lincoln Gate. A little way along Nassau Street, we escaped our captors and dived into a shop. David knew the proprietor, who kept the mob at bay. After an hour or so, we left and that was the end of the matter. Our hired suits lived to fight another day, that evening at an 'evening dress' dinner dance at Dublin Airport.

COLIN WILSON (1959)

At Commencements in 1942 (or 3), proceedings were interrupted by a shot being fired through one of the Examination Hall windows, behind the dais. On investigation of rooms in No. 1 or No. 2, the authorities found a student who was interested in firearms and had a partly assembled machine-gun in his rooms. I can't remember what happened after that!

PETER TICHER (1947)

A medical student, whom I shall call 'Y' because he is still around and mightn't like the publicity, had Rooms near the Examination Hall. While Commencements were in progress, from his rooms, he fired an air pistol through an open window, aiming at the ceiling. On striking the ceiling the pellets created a puff of plaster that fell on the audience below. It took a while before the Junior Dean (McDowell's predecessor) realised what was going on. When he did, action was swift because he had a shrewd suspicion who the culprit must be and 'Y' was sent down for a term.

COLIN WILSON (1959)

TRINITY 'CHARACTERS'

The college at that time shared many characters. One of these was Florence O'Sullivan Donaghue, a flamboyant figure who, at sixteen, started his student career brilliantly with a Double First. He claimed to be the illegitimate son of an earl, rarely had money and fleeced the tourists trooping in and out of college. Florry wore his hair unfashionably long and would approach Americans asking 'Spare a penny for a student's haircut?' It was infallible. Another odd figure was Dick Harris who claimed to be related to both Frank and 'Bomber' Harris – an unlikely combination – and though he appeared to be involved in college life and wandered around with a gown over his arm, the connection was obscure.

DR BRUMWELL HENDERSON CBE (1954)

I remember a marvellous sighting of McDowell's predecessor, also legendary, as, I think JD, then Senior Dean, R. M. Gwynn. Tall, very deaf, very good liberal Anglican theologian of famous literary family (Stephen Gwynn), whose brothers all converted to Rome. Anyway I caught him ambling across Front Square with the brother who was, I think, Professor of Modern History at UC Cork, each of them deploying in conversation small brass ear trumpets. Circa 1952. My time there.

W. L. (BILL) WEBB (1953)

Two of my wilder Trinity friends were Matthew, and James. Matthew's family owned a crumbling mansion and tracts of miry bog and moorland, in the West. I don't know anything of James's antecedents, but later he was reportedly involved in the fruit trade, into or out of, Tangier.

Towards the end of term, James was leaving on the Dublin-Liverpool boat and Matthew had come to see him off. They repaired to the bar, dark night came and neither heard the cry of 'All ashore that's going ashore.' The vessel cast off and moved towards the sea. Without hesitation, Matthew leapt, fully clad, and from a high deck, into the turbid Liffey, his only guide some few flickering lights on the quayside.

Hearing a bubbling cry of pain and the splash as he hit the icy water, some idlers had gathered. They were able to show our swimmer one of the vertical twelve foot ladders that ran down from the quay, to low tide level. No matter that the rungs were barnacle-infested and slippery with seaweed, hindering the ascent. Matthew mounted up, much encumbered by his water-logged overcoat. 'What will you take for the coat?' cried some wag. A Guard was now attracted to the commotion. 'One moment, Sir!' he commenced. 'No time for statements now' cried Matthew. At a brisk trot, dripping and festooned with seaweed, he made for a Pearse Street pub, for a very quick glass of hot whiskey before entering College by the Front Gate. 'Evening, McPherson' he cried to the open-mouthed porter, 'Cool, for the time of year.'

Telling the story later, James said that Matthew would never have jumped 'Only he had an important exam the next day.' Would that

I could tell you that he passed with flying colours. But no, he failed, dismally.

DR PETER DEMPSTER (1952)

When I was at Trinity in the late 1940s and for some years before and for some years after, there was another almost legendary figure with whom RB McDowell is sometimes compared. This was 'the Pope', or more precisely, Eoin O'Mahony, at that time a brief-less barrister of the Kings Inns. Any comparison is in most ways ridiculous for the two men could hardly have been more different. The Pope was a burly figure with a grey fringe of beard who only had to open his mouth to make it clear that he came from the far South West of Ireland. He spoke in a bold voice in an often quite pompous manner and, apart from having graduated a few years earlier than RB, he had no official position in Trinity; he simply enjoyed Trinity undergraduate parties, and it may have been at one of these that I met him. I personally have never thought of the Pope and RB as rival characters in any way. They were both parts of happy years at Trinity, but so different, even as raconteurs, that any comparison would have been invidious. I was intrigued that both at a later date were guests at Leixlip Castle, but Mariga Guinness could charm the birds off a tree.

HENRY CLARK (1950)

While – long, long ago:

Since we speak of an historian, herewith an historical anecdote: way back in the days of Town-and-Gown riots, there was a fighting Junior Dean, who led the student or gown faction in the forays. The leader of the townees, and the particular *bête noire* of that Junior Dean was a hefty butcher – and no love was lost between them.

One day a group of undergraduates had managed to separate this man from his minions and drag him into College. There in the way these things go, no one had any real idea of what to do next and the incident looked like to peter out, when the Junior Dean looked out of his window, probably attracted by the sound of the ruckus, and saw his arch enemy in the hands of the Collegians. He could not, of course, be seen to initiate any reprehensible course of conduct within the College precincts, but he was equal to the situation. He ran out into the Square crying 'Gentlemen! I beg you, whatever you do, do not nail that man's ears to the pump!' It needed only the time to produce the requisite hardware before the butcher was firmly so attached.

How unlike, how *very* unlike, the home life of our own dear Junior Dean!

MICHAEL BRERETON (1961)

The JD in Front Square c. 1966
© Chris Johnston

III ~ Recent Encounters with RB McDowell

19

RB McDowell:
I have always enjoyed both London and Dublin. In both there are good facilities for work and pleasure and they offer interesting contrasts in scale and tempo. When I am in London I soon become very much aware of the virtues of Dublin; back in Dublin within a short time, I am sighing for London.

London

REFORM CLUB

RB used to invite me to the University Club and to very grand houses. Later, when he was in London, I kept on meeting him in the Reform Club or the British Museum. He was a figure that appeared out of the blue, every so often.

RANDAL KINKEAD (1954)

PICCADILLY

My cousin and I were nearly knocked over by McDowell as he charged out of Piccadilly Tube Station in the late Seventies, early Eighties; we had a good laugh at the whirlwind!

HUGH WOODHOUSE (1970)

LONDON UNDERGROUND

I did, of course, read the book '*The Junior Dean – Encounters with a Legend*' and soon afterwards, one of those unnerving happenings occurred for I then met Dr McDowell in Piccadilly underground station one evening as he was making his way for a train. Dressed 'as usual' but unfazed by a stranger approaching him, he turned the conversation round and asked me how I was doing! As he disappeared down the escalators, having complained it had been a long day, I was struck by the thought that I only hope I am able to navigate the streets and Underground at such a great age. He, indeed, is a remarkable man!

STEPHEN RICHARDSON (1972)

I always remember the JD scuttling across Front Square when I was at TCD between 1966 and 1971, but, as a natural Scientist, I didn't know him. However, now I keep bumping into him at Green Park Tube Station, at Russell Square Tube Station, on the street, getting onto a bus, walking in front of me ... Uncanny! It happens day and night. Why is he in London?

ANN WALTER (1971) *[He lives there! Ed]*

Some years ago, McDowell acquired accommodation in a traditionally Irish region of North London. On being congratulated on having, at last, moved in with the Paddies, he responded '*Paddies, Paddies, not a Paddy to be seen, all Pakistanis and Indians, Tory voters to a man!*' Happily he now spends most of his time in Trinity holding forth on every topic in Commons or in the Kildare Street and University Club.

PROFESSOR TREVOR WEST (1960)
FELLOW, TRINITY COLLEGE, DUBLIN

INSTITUTE OF HISTORICAL RESEARCH

For many years, RB divided his time almost equally between London and Dublin. In London, he carried out research at the Institute of Historical Research and the London Library, frequently entertaining friends at The Reform Club.

However, in 2003 he wrote: 'It is pleasant to have attained ninety and people have been and are, most kind, but I am certainly finding the long London streets and transport problems very strenuous.'

Problems on London Transport continued all that year until the Tube strike in 2004 proved to be the final straw. Leaving the Reform Club, one evening, he found that there were neither trains nor taxis to be had and wrote, 'I had to fight my way on to a bus!' Thereafter he started to spend more time in Dublin, in his rooms in the Rubrics, walking daily to the University Club in St. Stephens Green:

20

Dublin

RETURN TO TRINITY

DAWSON STREET

I last met RB about a year ago when he was enjoying the hospitality of his cousin Harry McDowell and Harry's wife Joan at their home in Celbridge. In the course of conversation he remarked on his recent discovery that the walk from Trinity up Dawson Street to the Kildare Street and University Club was actually uphill. Age might have taken the spring from his step but his unique brand of humour, at once droll and perceptive, was clearly as lively as ever.

SIR RIVERS CAREW BT (1956)

Dr McDowell continues his writing and research in the Library and is frequently seen crossing Front Square to the delight of graduates for whom a return visit to College would not be complete without a glimpse of that familiar figure. DR RUTH BLACKALL (1954) *comments, 'It's a comfort to see him. Time has stood still.'*

THE MAGNIFICENT McDOWELL

RB returning to the Rubrics   © Richard Northbridge, 2004

21

Retirement – What Retirement?

This story took place on a day in 1995, when my daughter was an undergraduate in TCD, and I went with her to the offices of the History Department in the Arts Block, to see if some exam results were available. We were sitting in an outer office, where there were secretaries, as I recall, when a door opened from an inner room, and a slightly agitated-looking member of the academic staff appeared and as he did so, a familiar voice could be heard in full flow from the inner room. The door closed, the lecturer hurried as a man late for an important engagement, and the voice was heard no more. Some minutes later, exactly the same sequence was repeated, and again the lecturer hastened away, the door closed, and the voice was heard no more. A little while later, a third harassed-looking lecturer, late to give a lecture, appeared, but was this time followed into the outer office by Dr McDowell, clearly keen to finish the point he was making before losing the last member of his audience. Dr McDowell had lost none of his vigour, despite his alleged retirement.

DR FRANCIS SHEEHY SKEFFINGTON (1967)

22

The New Boat

*In 1952, during the Trinity Week Regatta, RB McDowell coxed
his crew to an historic victory at Islandbridge.
Fifty-three years later, another unusual Boat Club event took
place, this time in a floodlit Front Square:*

On a cold and windy November evening, Front Square is just slightly
less lugubrious than the river at Islandbridge. This is why members
of the Dublin University Boat Club, based there, decided on an
unusual switch. Instead of inviting Dr. R.B. McDowell to come to
the river to christen their new eight-oared shell, the shell was brought
to Dr. McDowell, only feet away from his rooms in the Rubrics at
the bottom of Front Square.

Beautifully displayed on trestles, with a DUBC scarf covering
her name, this new ship awaited the arrival of her name-giver. Dr.
McDowell soon appeared. He took the Club's challenge cup with
Liffey water from DUBC captain Edward Roffe-Silvester and
performed the christening ceremony, wishing good speed to all who
row in her. Meanwhile the removal of the scarf revealed the name
"R.B. McDowell."

Following this fine moment, the captain invited Dr. McDowell
and members and friends of the Club to champagne in his rooms

in Botany Bay. Difficult to say how many students' rooms RB must have visited during his life at Trinity but unchanged was his interest in those around him or his appetite for bisquity bites prepared so tastefully by the captain's various ladies.

Dr. McDowell is well aware of the frequent use now made of this fine boat, in training as well as racing, and at one of the Club's traditional dinners spoke of the close relationship between man and boat: *"She's like me, young, slender and fast."*

ROB VAN MESDAG (1951)

Rob van Mesdag, President, DUBC,
introduces Dr McDowell

© *Rob van Mesdag*

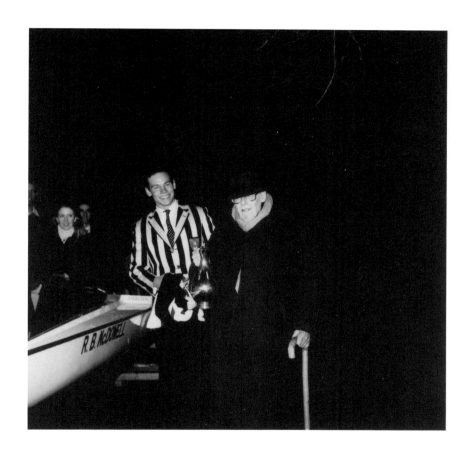

RB prepares to name the new boat
(l to r) Edward Roffe-Sylvester (Captain) RB McDowell
© Rob van Mesdag

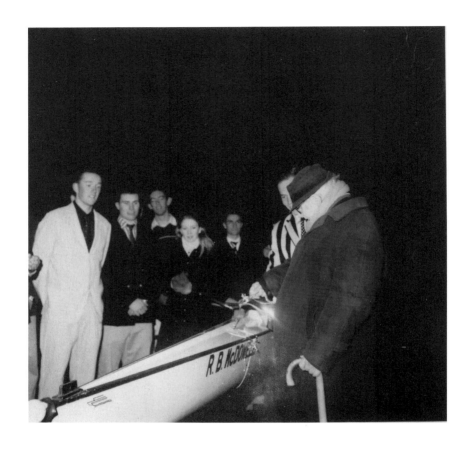

Dr McDowell christens the 'RB McDowell'
(l to r) Members of DUBC, Edward Roffe-Sylvester (Captain),
RB McDowell
© Rob van Mesdag

Toasting the new boat
Dr RB McDowell, Rob van Mesdag (President), Dr Sean Barratt
© Charles Larkin

THE MAGNIFICENT McDowell

Manuscripts Room, Trinity College Dublin
Presenting the original letters for The Junior Dean, to the Library ~ Anne Leonard, RB McDowell
© Pauline Brereton (Goodbody)

23

'The Junior Dean – Encounters with a Legend'

READERS' REVIEWS

RB McDowell
The number of people who have commented, and have read the book, is quite incredible.

A book to treasure and to take down if one is feeling a bit depressed. Indeed, at any time.
SIR WILLIAM DOUGHTY (1953)

I have enjoyed a day-long nostalgia trip.
DR RICHARD BRYN (1963)

Lovely book, lovely job!
TERENCE BRADY (1961)

What a marvellous evocation of vanished days.
DAVID GILLIAT (1961)

The book is the perfect rendering of my own memories of Trinity as a totally mythic sort of place, with the Junior Dean its most accomplished symbol
DR RICHARD STACK (1962)

I have simply been unable to put down your wonderful book about the JD. It is a triumph!
DR GILBERT HOWE (1964)

I read the book with a mixture of interest, amusement and nostalgia. All Trinity Graduates, who love eccentrics and value eccentricity, are in your debt.

REV. H. BARKLEY WALLACE (1956)

It brings back many fond memories of the JD and of the hallowed precincts of TCD.

NIGEL EVES (1971)

The Junior Dean is a testament to RB McDowell's deeper social success which was his talent for engaging with the undergraduates – at their parties and in their student debates.

ERIC WAUGH (1952)

The tributes from the contributors I knew seem to be precisely in keeping with the characters who wrote them. It was like being in touch with old friends again whom I had not seen for 40 years.

JOSE XUEREB (1963)

Trinity still features prominently in my thoughts and the anecdotes have brought back many happy memories of my time there in the Medical School from 1965 to 1971.

DR SIMON BUTLER (1971)

I could almost feel the cobbles of the Front Square under my feet.

DR CHRISTOPHER PETIT (1956)

A valiant masterpiece of merriment.

CHARLES SWEETING (1950)

A hoot!

JOHN WYSE JACKSON

Advice

I do get a bit little tired of good natured but lazy remarks. I get very tired of being asked 'Are you well?' You see, if you are up and about they can assume, if you are at Piccadilly, you are not dangerously ill! On the other hand, at my age it's not likely you are absolutely 100%. The obvious thing to say is 'You look well.'

And finally:

'The people who knew the best stories about me are all dead!'
DR RB McDOWELL

𝕴ncidentals Account with 𝕿rinity College.

Quarter ending 31 March 1958.

Tutor,................................4.......................................

Name,...................C. B. Wilson...........................

	£	s.	d.
Commons Fund . . .	6	2	6
Chamber Rent . . .	7	0	0
Gas	1	4	7
Electricity . . .		13	4
* Servant	6	3	6
Milk	1	9	10
Repairs and Dilapidations .			
* Registration of Chambers .			
Punishments . . .			
* Baths		5	0
* Garage Rent . . .			
Total, £	22	18	9

This account should be paid *direct to the Bank of Ireland, College Green, Dublin*, on or before **Saturday, 12 April 1958.** For tardy payment a fine of 2s. 6d. per day is imposed and should be included in the amount of the payment made.

On 21 April the rooms of students still in default will be declared vacant.

N.B.—Items marked with an asterisk are calculated for the period 1 January to 31 March, rent for the period 1 April to 30 June and other items for the period 18 November to 17 February.

Please complete the enclosed form and return it to the Bank of Ireland.

College Expenses, 1958

Index of Contributors

CONTRIBUTOR	TCD GRADUATION	ADDRESS	PAGE
Dr Sean Barratt	-	Dublin	9
Michael Bloch	-	London	2
The Hon. Andrew Bonar Law	1959	Dublin	101, 112
Dr Ruth Blackall	1954	London	127
Terence Brady	1961	Somerset	1, 46, 117, 137
Michael Brereton	1961	Dublin	17, 23, 31, 32, 34, 37, 40, 47, 111, 115-116, 124
Pauline Brereton (Goodbody)	1961	Dublin	20
Martin Byrne	1963	Cheshire	100
Vincent Byrne	1956	Staffs	81-83, 106
Dr Richard Byrn	1963	Yorkshire	13, 26, 137
Charles Burrowes	1949	Co Down	44
Dr Simon Butler	1969	Cheshire	138
Sir Rivers Carew Bt.	1956	Cambridge	17, 84, 127
Marjorie Chambers (Douglas)	1962	Co Down	22
Henry Clark	1950	Wiltshire	1, 66, 69, 98, 123
Dr John Connor	1958	Nova Scotia	28, 35, 108
Joe Conneally *(The Irish Times)*	1981	Dublin	11, 58
Rev Charles Cooke	1954	Nottingham	23, 27
Alan Cook	1955	Dublin	11
Dr Peter Dempster	1952	Dublin	62, 85, 120, 123
Sir William Doughty	1953	Bucks	137
Nigel Eves	1971	Co Down	138
Dr I.K. Ferguson OBE	1964	Glos.	103
Derek Fielding	1952	Queensland	24, 48, 93
F M Foley	1937	Hampshire	13
Professor Michael Foot CBE,TD	-	Herts	2, 57

Glossary

Ad eundum	Reciprocal recognition of BA and MA examinations at Trinity, Oxford and Cambridge
Bluebottle	The porter who announced the Scholar who was to call Grace in Commons
Board	Governing body of the university consisting of the Provost, the Fellows and the Scholars
Book of Kells	9th Century illuminated manuscript. Kept in TCD since 1660.
Botany Bay	'The Bay'; one of three spacious squares containing accommodation units known as 'Rooms.' Completed in 1817. Originally contained a herb garden.
Campanile	Bell tower in Front Square, built c. 1850.
Chanter	Read the lessons in the College Chapel.

Commencements	Ceremony when Degrees are conferred.
Commons	Meal served in the 18TH Century Dining Hall, a tradition of community that has existed almost since the foundation of the College. The Provost & Fellows, Scholars & Sizars dine without charge.
GMB	Graduates' Memorial Building. Finest neo Gothic building in Ireland. Home of The Hist. and The Phil.
Gardaí	The Irish Police Force
Grace	Repeated *a memoriter* by a Scholar 'before and after meat.'

'At Commons in the Dining Hall, according to ancient usage, grace shall be said both before and after meals by one of the Scholars or students appointed for the purpose by the Board, and in the following form:

GRACE BEFORE MEAT
'Oculi Omnium in te sperant Domine. Tu das iis escam eorum in tempore opportuno. Aperis tu manum tuam, et imples omne animal benedictione tua. Miserere nostri te quaesumus Domine, tuisque donis quae de tua benignitate sumus percepturi, benedicito per Christum Dominum nostrum' Amen.

GRACE AFTER MEAT

'Tibi laus, tibi honor, tibi Gloria, O beata et gloriosa Trinitas. Sit nomen Domini benedictum et nunc et in perpetuum. Laudamus te, benignissime Pater, pro serenissimis, regina Elizabetha hujus Collegii conditrice, Jacobo ejusdem munificentissimo auctore, Carolo conservatore, caeterisque benefactoribus nostris, rogantes te, ut his tuis donis recte et ad tuam gloriam utentes in hoc saeculo, te una cnm fidelibus in futuro feliciter perfruamur, per Christum Dominum nostrum.' Amen.

Grinds
Private Tuition

'The Hist.'
Debating society, founded in 1770, in which, it was claimed, 'great public figures learned to hone their oratorical skills'. Originally, 'Burke's Debating Club'. Situated in the Graduates Memorial Building (GMB), the Hist is the oldest student debating society in the world.

Honors
Latinate designation for an Honours Degree, still in use.

'The JD'
Dr RB McDowell

Junior Dean
College officer responsible for enforcing discipline and dealing with accommodation in College.

Knights of the Campanile
Established in 1926 to entertain visiting Oxford and Cambridge teams. The

tie is pink for Trinity, dark blue for Oxford, light blue for Cambridge.

Library

One of only six copyright libraries in the British Isles. The library's right to claim a copy of all books and periodicals, maps and sheet music published in the UK and Ireland is enshrined by Charter in both countries.

Little-go

Examination for Honors students at the end of their Senior Freshman year. Arts undergraduates took two scientific subjects and science undergraduates, two arts subjects. Discontinued in 1959.

Long Room (of the Library)

Dates from 1732. Described as 'one of the most spectacular spaces in Ireland', this is the oldest single chamber library in the world. Contains about 200,000 of the library's oldest books including the Book of Kells.

Moderatorship

'Mod.' Honors degree. Four years to complete.

'The Phil'

University Philosophical Society, founded in 1853. Situated in the Graduates Memorial Building (the GMB), the Phil is the oldest paper-reading society in the world.

Pinks

University Colours (Pink was Elizabeth I's racing colour). Awarded to outstanding sportsmen and women at national and international level.

Players	Dublin University Players: the college amateur dramatic society which had a theatre at No 3, Front Square. Productions ran for two weeks and were reviewed by the Press.
Porter	'Guinness' which was brewed, originally, to suit the tastes of local Dublin porters.
The Porters	On duty at the Porters Lodge, they worked for the Junior Dean, performing a huge number of tasks relating to good order within the precincts.
Reader	Cleric taking the service in College Chapel, who chanted.
Reading Room	Octagonal reading room built in 1937. In use during the Golden Era.
Rooms	Four hundred and fifty sets of sitting rooms and bedrooms in College. Until 1972, only available to male undergraduates.
Rubrics	Trinity's oldest surviving building. Built c. 1700. Contains sets of rooms for students and staff.
'Schol'	Competitive scholarship examination, open to all undergraduates, in their second year.
Scholars	Undergraduates who become members of the body corporate of the College. Awards announced by the Provost on Trinity Monday.

Second Grace	Grace after meat.
Sizar	Recipient of a scholarship received on entering college.
Skip	College domestic servant
Trinity Monday	First day of 'Trinity Week' on which the Provost announces the names of the new Fellows and Scholars.
Trinity News	Ireland's oldest student newspaper. In circulation since 1947.
Trinity Week	Takes place in June when there are a number of social and sporting events culminating in the famous Trinity Ball
'Wife'	Person sharing College rooms
Junior Freshman	First year undergraduate
Senior Freshman	Second year undergraduate
Junior Sophister	Third year undergraduate
Senior Sophister	Fourth year undergraduate
Michaelmas Term	Christmas Term (October, November and December)
Hilary Term	Spring Term (January, February, March)
Trinity Term	Summer Term (March, April, May)